THE
TRINITY GUIDE
TO THE
CHRISTIAN CHURCH

THE
TRINITY GUIDE
TO THE
CHRISTIAN
CHURCH

William J. La Due

continuum
NEW YORK • LONDON
www.continuumbooks.com

Continuum, 80 Maiden Lane, New York, NY 10038

Continuum, The Tower Building, 11 York Road, London SE1 7NX

Cover design: Jennifer Glosser

Library of Congress Cataloging-in-Publication Data
La Due, William J.
  The Trinity guide to Christian church / William J. La Due.
     p. cm.
  Includes bibliographical references and index.
  ISBN-13: 978-0-8264-1950-7 (pbk.)
  ISBN-10: 0-8264-1950-X
1. Church—History of doctrines. 2. Church. I. Title.
  BV598.L28 2006
  262.009—dc22
                                        2006019627

Printed in the United States of America

06 07 08 09 10   10 9 8 7 6 5 4 3 2 1

To the church of God that is in Corinth,
to those who are sanctified in Christ Jesus,
called to be saints,
together with all those who in every place
call on the name of our Lord Jesus Christ,
both their Lord and ours:
Grace to you and peace from God our Father
and the Lord Jesus Christ.

1 Corinthians 1:2–3

CONTENTS

INTRODUCTORY NOTE

World-shaking ideas require embodiment if they are to survive beyond their first or second generation. The same is true of the Christian ethos. The endlessly intriguing figure of Christ would not have endured from century to century unless his splendid memory had been preserved by the Christian churches. The forms and shapes of church have been and continue to be varied, and this constitutes one of the most remarkable tributes to the genius of Jesus of Nazareth, who is truly the God-man for all seasons.

This small study attempts to trace some of the more notable embodiments of the legacy of Christ, who continues to find his way into new societal incarnations through which to be present among humankind. From the house churches of the first generations, from the breathtaking medieval cathedrals and the hallowed lecture rooms of the universities, to the unadorned prayer hall of Azusa Street in Los Angeles, the cradle of the Pentecostals, there is Jesus among his people, inspiring, teaching, and engaging them with his undying love.

Let me add my most sincere thanks to Henry L. Carrigan Jr., my faithful publisher, who continues to believe in my work, and to Amy Wagner, my gifted senior managing editor. Finally, I want to express my profound gratitude to my dear wife, Margaret, who has been my daily companion and my chief source of encouragement throughout this project.

1

THE EARLIEST
DEVELOPMENTS

Original Models of Church in the New Testament

Several years ago in a book on the Roman papacy, I referred to various original models of the church as reflected in the New Testament.[1] The first of these could be considered the paradigm of the Apostle Paul, who visited and evangelized in such cities as Colossae, Philippi, and Corinth. On occasion, he would begin his mission in the Jewish synagogues, and at other times he would conduct his preaching in the homes of those who had been previously converted to the Christian message. These private residences, which were larger than the average dwellings, could be considered the first churches where believers would gather to worship, pray, and receive instructions. In the larger cities—like Rome and Antioch in Syria—there could well have been a dozen or more of these house churches. Stephanas of Corinth (1 Cor 1:16), Philemon of Colossae (Phlm 1, 2), and Aquila and Prisca in Corinth (Acts 18:1–3) provided their residences for worship in their communities.

As Paul moved on, he would keep in contact with these churches by means of letters and/or emissaries. Individuals identified as prophets and teachers who were lifted up by the Holy Spirit provided the leadership in these congregations. Ministers of this sort apparently functioned for a time, and then they normally returned to their previous places in the general congregation. Neither Rome nor Corinth, for example, seemed for a number of years to have any fixed offices. In fact, it was not until Paul's Letter to the Philippians (ca. 56–60) that there is any mention of overseers and ministers with any set function. Those who were the owners of the house churches (in which twenty to fifty congregants would gather for worship) do not seem to have had any fixed powers of governance, but they were probably the ones who more closely resemble what could be called church officials.

The Apostle Paul spoke of those who "labor among you and have charge of you in the Lord, and admonish you" (1 Thess 5:12), but these

1

do not seem to relate to fixed or stable positions. This reference is likely to refer to intermittent service roles within the congregations. In general, the organizational pattern in the Pauline churches appears to be rather informally structured, with great dependence on the regular influence of the Holy Spirit. Paul understood that each believer was empowered to provide gifts for other members of the communities.

The Jerusalem congregation as described by Luke in Acts was cared for by the Twelve, who provided the preaching and the worship functions but delegated the charitable duties to "seven men of good standing"—considered in the tradition to be the first deacons (Acts 6:3). Luke describes the distinct roles of the Twelve (9:1–6) and of the seventy-two (10:1–12). However, neither Luke's gospel nor Acts provides much information as to how the primitive communities were structured, or who exercised authority over the congregations. Acts 15:2 indicates the role of presbyters or elders as sharing responsibilities with the apostles in Jerusalem. Soon after the Council of Jerusalem (ca. 49), the apostles apparently took their leave of Jerusalem, and the control of the original congregation was left to James the brother of the Lord and the elders. Luke, however, does make an effort to portray the various churches of the first and second generations as having a somewhat uniform organizational structure. For example, he was fond of describing Paul's churches with a presbyterial arrangement that in all likelihood they did not possess.

As described by Luke, although the college of presbyters frequently lacked a leader (Acts 20:28–30), they were the administrators of the congregations and possessed shepherding functions over the faithful. The Gospel of Matthew contains hardly any reference to the local administration of the churches. There were teachers, and in some cases prophets (7:15–20), but the organization of the communities was quite informal. There is no local administration clearly in evidence nor is there reference even to a group of elders in the congregation. The promise to Peter recorded in Matthew 16 did not seem to provide him with an unambiguous position of leadership either in Antioch, where he resided for some years, or in Rome. The so-called "ecclesiastical" gospel leaves us with little information concerning Matthew's congregations. According to the Gospel and the other writings of John, discipleship seems to be the most critical function, but there is hardly any evidence of hierarchical organization. The only exception seems to be in the short Third Letter of John, which alludes to a residential authority in one of the communities, and to a presbyter who exercises a responsibility of some sort over several of these congregations. The significance of the passage (3 John 1:9–10) is much disputed and fails to shed any probative light on the organization of the Johannine churches. It is the Holy Spirit who directs the life of the churches (John 14:15–17), but the most important issue is the relationship between the individual believer and Jesus through the Spirit.

The Pastoral Epistles, 1 and 2 Timothy and Titus, are held by many to have been written after the death of Paul (ca. 64). They can more likely be dated between 80 and 125 and reflect the churches' organization at a much later date, when bishops and presbyters presided over the congregations. Ordination seems to be called for in the case of some of the office-holders (1 Tim 4:14). Throughout the period of the New Testament, there was indeed much variation in terms of church order and discipline. Yet, as Hans von Campenhausen notes, "The pastoral epistles do not bear witness to a canon law which is only beginning, but to one already fairly well developed. . . ."[2] However, within the organizational patterns of the late first- and early-second-century Christian churches, there is much variation in discipline. As a matter of fact, the New Testament evidence for a plurality of confessions ". . . has not been sufficiently reckoned with . . . , and its possible corollaries for modern denominational diversity need to be thought through with greater care and thoroughness."[3]

Early Christian Fathers

According to the letter of the Romans to the Corinthians (1 Clem.), written in 95 or 96, one of the earliest Christian documents outside the New Testament, the system of presbyters, which dates from the apostles, was the usual form of church organization in Syria, Asia Minor, and Rome. First Clement makes clear that this organizational pattern in many of the local churches was considered part of the constitutional fabric of the young church. The letters of St. Ignatius of Antioch to the churches in Asia Minor (ca. 110) reveal that a monarchical bishop was in charge of the congregations at Ephesus, Magnesia, Tralles, Philadelphia, and Smyrna. This was not the case, however, in Rome, where the church was apparently governed by the elders or presbyters. In fact, the Roman congregation did not seem to have a monarchical bishop until about the middle of the second century.

A Christian scholar from the East named Hegesippus visited Rome around 160 and remained there for some twenty years. He revealed that Anicetus was the Roman monarchical bishop circa 155 to 166. He noted that Soter had succeeded Anicetus and was then followed by the monarchical bishop Eleutherus (ca. 174–189), who was the reigning bishop when Hegesippus left Rome and returned to the East. His efforts to reestablish the succession of bishops in Rome and elsewhere were aimed at refuting the gnostics, who insisted that the secret revelations of the gnostic teachers were the most important sources of the Christian tradition.

Hegesippus and Irenaeus of Lyons (ca. 140–after 200) maintained that the handing down of sacred doctrine from bishop to bishop in the apostolic sees was the most reliable source of the teachings of Jesus.

The battle against the gnostic heresy continued for many decades, although the influence of the heresy was strongest in the second century. The heretic Marcion—who came to Rome circa 140—was probably the most formidable gnostic opponent, although his teachings did not include many of the bizarre theories of his co-believers. In spite of the fact that Marcion left Rome in 144, he remained a dangerous opponent. Toward the end of the third century, the influence of Gnosticism began to wane, and in the fourth century, it was reduced to relative insignificance.[4]

The church in the first two centuries lived with a good many structural and theological differences from one congregation to the other. Although the monarchical episcopate was becoming more prevalent, there were still congregations in which the controlling authority resided in the presbyterate, which had not yet been placed under the control of a monarchical head. From place to place there were differences in church organization and even in doctrinal emphasis, but these differences did not affect the communion that existed among the various churches. The historian Gregory Dix has noted that even in the second and third centuries in Rome there were theological positions expounded by some authorized teachers that were quite diverse, and it was only when a certain mentor demonstrated beyond all doubt that his doctrine differed notably in essentials from the officially recognized Roman creed that the presbyters (or the monarchical bishop) felt the need to expel this teacher from communion.[5] Thus, it can be concluded that there was indeed a certain variety in doctrine and discipline among the various Christian congregations in the second and third centuries, and yet this variety did not seem to be an obstacle to communion among these churches. The monarchical episcopate was becoming more widespread, but there were still congregations in which the controlling authority resided in the presbyterate that did not yet possess a monarchical head.

During the persecutions of the Roman emperors Decius (249–51) and Gallus (251–53), Bishop Cyprian of Carthage (d. 258) was engaged in a bitter struggle with Pope Stephen (254–57), the bishop of Rome, over the question of the need to re-baptize those who had fallen away during the recent persecutions. The practice in Rome was simply to readmit those who had fallen away by means of the recitation of the creed and the imposition of hands. However, Cyprian and the bishops of North Africa insisted that those who had defected be re-baptized. Thus, their pastoral practice in this regard was quite different. Cyprian was convinced that "every appointed leader has in the government of the church the freedom to exercise his own judgment and will, while one day having to render an account of his conduct to the Lord."[6] A jurisdictional authority above the local bishop—an authority to command in terms of discipline and even in teaching—did not seem to exist in the mind of Cyprian and in the practice of the mid-third-century church. The local bishop at this time was largely answerable to no one but God. Although regional councils were being held in certain areas, for example, in North Africa, the local bishops were not absolutely bound by the regional enactments. The decisions in the local diocese were not generally subject to a higher ecclesiastical authority. Thus, the subordination of the local ordinary to a higher jurisdictional power was quite uncommon in the third century. Once appointed and installed, the local bishop could consider himself answerable only to God.

In a letter to Cyprian, Bishop Fermilian of Caesarea in Cappadocia affirmed the following:

> And anyone can see that those who are in Rome do not observe in all particulars those things that were handed down from the beginning; it is pointless, therefore, for them to parade the authority of the apostles. . . . This is as we find in very many other provinces: there is a great deal of diversity just as the people and the places themselves vary. And yet there does not follow from this that there has been any departure at all from the peace and unity of the Catholic Church.[7]

In his treatise *The Unity of the Catholic Church*, probably written in 251, Cyprian taught that although Peter received the power of the keys before the other apostles, the very same power held by Peter was conferred upon the others. The only difference was that Peter received his authority a short time before the other apostles.[8] Cyprian's position was somewhat ambiguous, but he does not seem to allow for the existence of a direct jurisdictional power over the local ordinary, even on the part of the Roman pontiff.

The first ecumenical council at Nicaea (325) directed that the bishops of each province were to take part in the selection and ordination of a new bishop in their province, and the proceedings were to be confirmed by the metropolitan bishop.[9] The authority of the bishops of Rome, Alexandria, Antioch, and Jerusalem was recognized in canons 6 and 7, but their prerogatives were not enumerated. The pattern of the five patriarchs was beginning to appear and followed the development of the prerogatives of the metropolitans. At the Council of Serdica, which opened in the fall of 343, a precedent was established for appeals to the pope when a local bishop felt that he had been unjustly treated by his metropolitan. This practice of appealing to the Roman pontiff became more and more popular in the West, but the procedure never gained much currency among the churches of the East.

The Church—East and West

By the year 400 or thereabouts, the area of the Roman Empire around the Aegean Sea was the most heavily populated, and Asia Minor apparently contained the greatest number of Christians. Although there were some sizable Christian congregations in Italy, Spain, Gaul, and northern Africa, the majority of Christian adherents were in the East. During the fourth and fifth centuries, the growth of Christianity was phenomenal. The western emperor, Valentinian III (425–55), did much to elevate the prestige of the pope in the West, but his efforts had little effect in the East.

Pope Damasus (366–84), Pope Siricius (384–99), and Pope Leo (440–61) occasionally attempted to exercise the same authority over the East that they wielded in the West, but they were not successful. At the Council of Constantinople in 381, the delegates wished to grant to the bishop of Constantinople the same prerogatives that were enjoyed by the Roman pontiff, but this was never sanctioned by the pope.[10] The important canon 28 was strongly rejected by Pope Leo I as contrary to the venerable traditions of Nicaea. Although the popes were acquiring more jurisdiction over the provinces in the West, the Eastern churches continued to retain their primary allegiance to their respective patriarchs.

The 850 or more extant official letters of Pope Gregory I (590–604) give us a marvelous picture of the organizational arrangement in the church at the beginning of the seventh century. His control over the western regions such as Sicily, Rimini, Ravenna, and Milan was direct and largely undisputed, while his authority in the churches of North Africa, Dalmatia, and the Balkans was more a matter of moral suasion rather than direct jurisdiction. The patriarchs of Constantinople, Alexandria, Antioch, and Jerusalem were for the most part the pope's equals within their respective territories. The Roman pontiff almost invariably addressed the four other patriarchs in a fraternal tone, for he saw them as his equals. There was, however, a special bond of unity among the sees of Antioch, Alexandria, and Rome, because these centers were more intimately related to Peter. According to Pope Gregory, Peter presided over the see of Antioch for seven years and sent the evangelist Mark to Alexandria. After his sojourn in Antioch, Peter resided in Rome until his death in 64–68. These three sees were for Pope Gregory actually one: The one Petrine see was actualized in three locations. Gregory normally addressed the other four patriarchs as brothers and did not see himself as their superior because they were to guide and direct the universal church together.

After Gregory, the East and the West drifted apart over the next several centuries. There were a number of reasons for the separation. The invasion of the Muslims in the East occupied most of the attention and resources of the Orientals, while the battle over the cult of icons further alienated the East from the West in the eighth century. Moreover, the Roman emperor in Constantinople, Leo III (717–41), ordered the confiscation of all papal states in Calabria and Sicily and transferred all the Balkan regions under the jurisdiction of the patriarch of Constantinople. These moves deeply affected the papacy's income and prestige.[11]

Meanwhile, in Italy, Pope Gregory II (715–31) and Pope Gregory III (731–41) were having serious problems with the Lombards in northern and central Italy. After the Lombards occupied Ravenna in the late 730s, Gregory III decided that he would have to look to Charles Martel and the Franks for protection. This shift of allegiance from Constantinople to the Frankish kingdom altered the relationship between East and West dramatically. From that point, the popes' attention shifted to the West, and communication with the East and the eastern patriarchs began to wane. Popes Gregory II and Gregory III were largely responsible for easing the papal domain out of the Byzantine Empire.[12] As mentioned previously, although the drift apart was caused by actions both of the popes and of the emperors in Constantinople, the separation of East and West had begun in the eighth century. Byzantium was troubled with its own challenges, and the popes had to seek military protection where they could find it. The gradual amalgamation of the papal patrimonies in Italy in the eighth century resulted in the development of a nation-state that came to be known as the Papal States. As Geoffrey Barraclough has indicated:

> At no time in the whole preceding history of the papacy had there been any suggestion that the bishop of Rome should exercise temporal power, or rule like a king over a territorial state. If this claim was now made, it was, no doubt, in response to a peculiarly difficult situation. But the claim, once made, was never dropped. It runs like a red thread through papal history right down to the Lateran treaties of 1929 . . . and influenced the very character of the papacy itself.[13]

The Byzantine historian George Ostrogorsky had this to say regarding the relationship between East and West after the coronation of Charlemagne by Pope Leo III in the year 800: "[F]rom the year 800 onwards the two empires, an eastern and a western, stood face to face. . . .

The OIKOUMENE [i.e., the universal Christian world] had split into two halves which in language, culture, politics, and religion were poles apart."[14] The pentarchy, that is, the coordinated rule of the five great patriarchs, was implicit in several of the early ecumenical councils from 381–680, and served as the backdrop regarding ecclesiastical matters for the legislation of the Roman Emperor Justinian (527–65): "Authentic ecumenicity required the participation of these five patriarchs either in person or by proxy. . . . This system of 'pentarchy', the governing of the universal church by five rulers, equal in dignity, but related to one another by a strict order of precedence, was a Byzantine vision, enshrined in the legislation of Justinian."[15] This ecclesiastical order was formally proposed as an organizational pattern by such later Eastern scholars as Theodore the Studite (759–826).

In the ninth century, Archbishop Hincmar of Rheims stressed the role of metropolitans, which was increasing in importance in the West as a second tier of administration between the local bishop and the papacy. Hincmar did not view the church by any means as a papal monarchy, but rather as a communion of congregations united through their bishops and through a common faith. In Hincmar's view, the role of the bishop of Rome was to apply the canons of the major councils in the light of historical circumstances. The pontiff was not to legislate, but rather to apply the conciliar norms to the needs and the conditions of the time. The metropolitans, that is, the ordinaries of the major sees of Christendom, were to make sure that the conciliar enactments of the great and regional councils were followed in their territories and implemented by the bishops of their provinces. (Eastern metropolitans operated within the authority of the four Eastern patriarchs.)

Popes Nicholas I (858–67), Hadrian II (867–72), and John VIII (872–82) lost sight of the pentarchy and fashioned a system of church governance under the sole authority of the Roman pontiff. Pope Nicholas I conceived the whole church as a single people under the rule of the Roman pontiff, grounded on the rather unique theology of Pope Gelasius I (494–96). This vision was certainly not shared by the Eastern churches, for their organizational paradigm remained that of the pentarchy. Pope Nicholas I, in a letter to the Emperor Michael in 865, described papal jurisdiction as being supreme and universal, subject to the divine judgment alone; all ecclesiastical decisions are subject to the ultimate authority of the pope.[16] Pope Hadrian II understood the church to be a single *societas* over which the pope presided.[17] John VIII insisted that the Roman church holds the chief place over all churches. In the minds of these pontiffs, there was no longer any room for a pentarchy of five equal patriarchs sharing the responsibility for the governance of the whole church.

The Crisis in 1054

The pope's jurisdictional claims spanned the entire Christian world, but this vision was quite foreign to the Eastern patriarchs and their adherents. In the summer of 1054, two events fractured the tenuous union between East and West, which had been drifting apart for centuries. The solemn excommunication levied against Patriarch Michael Cerularius of Constantinople and his companions by the papal legates and the corresponding excommunication of the Roman legates by Patriarch Cerularius precipitated the formal division between East and West. However, it was not recognized for what it was either in the East or in the West until the Crusades, which for two hundred years spread a spirit of hatred and antagonism down to the level of common folk. In spite of numerous efforts to unify the Christian world over the centuries, East and West are still divided, perhaps permanently.

The first notable separations in the unity of the OIKOUMENE occurred with the Nestorians, who moved out of the Byzantine Empire in the late fifth century and settled in Persia, finding a home in the Persian church. The Nestorians held to two distinct persons in Christ, the divine and the human. Their position was condemned as heretical at the Council of Ephesus in 431, which declared that although Christ has two natures, human and divine, he is one person, the person of the Word. This doctrine was affirmed at the Council of Chalcedon (451). The Monophysites were the main group opposing this position; they insisted that there was only one nature in Christ, which was either divine or a blend of the divine and the human. Christians in Syria and in Egypt were for the most part Monophysites. The missionary activity of the Monophysites went southward and formed the Coptic patriarchate of Egypt, while the Nestorians in Persia continued to press on eastward toward India and even to China. Due to the heroic efforts of the Monophysite missionary Jacob Baradai (d. 578), the Monophysites firmly established themselves in Syria and among the Arabs of the Syrian desert. These divisions lessened the influence of the Orthodox of the Chalcedonian persuasion in Africa and also in the East.

In the sixth century, the Byzantine Empire was attacked and invaded from the north by the Slavs and the Avars (a Hunnic people), who crossed the Danube and occupied large sections of the Balkan Peninsula. At the same time, the Persians were punishing the eastern provinces. Emperor Heraclius (610–41) reorganized the empire and fought back the Persians in the east—clearing out Asia Minor for the restoration of Byzantine rule. Heraclius defeated the invaders from the north, the Avars, at the Battle of Constantinople. In 638, six years after the death of Muhammad, the Arabs conquered Syria and Palestine, with Egypt falling soon thereafter.

The lands taken by the Persians were overrun by the Muslims within ten years of the death of the Prophet Muhammad.

During these hectic decades, the Byzantine Empire had little time to attend to the popes' problems with the Lombards in Italy. This occasioned the popes' shift of allegiance to Francia, which further deepened the alienation between East and West. At this time, the Greek language replaced Latin in the affairs of church and state in Constantinople, and this too widened the separation. Constantinople at this time truly considered the Western church as uncultured and almost bordering on barbarism. On the other hand, the papacy became more and more oblivious to the dynamics of the pentarchy (i.e., the rule of the five patriarchs) and began to fashion itself as the sole supreme shepherd of the entire church. The papacy began to identify itself as a monarchy, having little to do with the original Petrine office. The significant issues of government and doctrine, according to the paradigm of the pentarchy, were to be debated and settled among the five patriarchs, while matters of greatest importance were left to be decided within the context of an ecumenical council.

Another issue that precipitated a deepening of the rift between East and West was the dispute over the *filioque* formula, which was introduced into the creed in the sixth and seventh centuries in Spain and adopted in Francia in the late eighth century. In the early eleventh century, this found its way into the Roman creed. The Greeks have two objections to the formula. First, the change from *a Patre per Filium* to *Filioque* was made in the West without any consultation with the East. The more fundamental objection of the Orthodox, however, has to do with the nature of the change. According to most Orthodox theologians, the procession of the Holy Spirit is from the Father alone, and not from the Father and the Son. The unilateral modification of the creed of Nicaea-Constantinople appeared in the acts of the Third Regional Council of Toledo in 589 and was adopted later by the Frankish church. In Rome, the popes did not sanction the change until 1014. This meant that a solemn creedal formula from Constantinople I (381) was altered without discussing it with the East. The issue remains a major point of contention with the Orthodox.[18]

An additional major source of tension and division was created by the Crusades, especially the Fourth Crusade (1202–4). In April 1204, Constantinople was viciously sacked. This wanton destruction is judged to be "one of the most ghastly and tragic incidents in history."[19] Runciman adds:

> The Byzantines prided themselves, with justice, on their learning and culture. Now they saw their libraries going up in flames, with all the manuscripts of the ancient world and all their classical and contemporary works of art. More immediately horrifying were

the outrages committed on the men, women, and children of the city and on its priests, monks, and nuns. What shocked the godly East most deeply was the sacrilege done to the churches. . . . Not a church was spared. . . . But the price was the lasting enmity of Greek Christendom.[20]

What divided the East from the West was primarily "the hatred of the Greeks for the Latins provoked by the wrongs they had suffered."[21] Pelican adds:

At the Council of Lyons in 1274, the fourteenth ecumenical council by Western count, Byzantine representatives accepted reconciliation with the Latins. An even more auspicious attempt at reunion came in Florence in 1439, where the Eastern delegates and the Western spokesmen both made basic concessions. These two councils were bracketed by the Latin sack of Constantinople during the Fourth Crusade in 1204 and by the Turkish capture of Constantinople in 1453. The political forces represented by the two conquests of New Rome made the achievements of the two councils a hollow victory, and reunification was declared null and void both times.[22]

The last pope mentioned in the official records of the Orthodox church in Constantinople was John XVIII, who died in 1009. In the estimate of some, the year 1009 should mark the onset of the schism by Greek calculations. The heart of the matter rests on the issue of the unilateral modification of the creed.

The Creed had been issued by an Oecumenical Council, which was in Eastern eyes the one inspired doctrinal authority. To add to the Creed was to question the authority and inspiration of the Fathers of the Church. Only another Oecumenical Council has the right not indeed to alter, but to amplify and explain the decisions reached at an earlier council. If the Western Churches tampered unilaterally with the Creed of the councils they must thereby automatically lapse into heresy; nor would any pronouncement by the Pope in their favor serve to condone them. The East saw in the dispute a direct attack on its whole theory of Church government and doctrine.[23]

The frustrated efforts toward unity at Lyons II (1274) and at Florence (1439) were never accepted by the people and the clergy of the East. In

1869, Pius IX invited the bishops of the Eastern Orthodox churches to the sessions of Vatican I (1869–70), but they refused to attend due to his previous history with the Orthodox and his lack of sensitivity to the traditions of the Eastern churches. Vatican II (1962–65) also invited delegates from the Orthodox churches, and in November 1964 it published its *Decree on the Eastern Churches*, which proclaims the equality of the Eastern traditions with the traditions of the West. However, "the Decree remains a Latin text about the Eastern tradition."[24] Much must be done in a bilateral way, to open the doors and deepen the dialogue between East and West.

Stress Lines in the West from 1100

Signs of discontent and division in the Western church began to appear in the twelfth century. From roughly 1100 onward, the regional character of church organization in the West began to give way to a widespread centralizing tendency, which gradually deprived the local churches of authority over major clerical appointments, decision-making, and discipline, which they had enjoyed for one thousand years. By means of the papal reservation of appointments to higher local offices and the evolution of the papal law courts, more and more decisions were being made by the pope's curia. Due to this expansion of administrative and judicial authority in the papal offices, funds to support the rapidly growing bureaucracy had to be collected from the local churches through additional taxes and fees of various sorts. In many instances, the curia provided a faster and more definitive set of solutions to local problems through its power to dispense from the established norms and to give irrevocable solutions to many pastoral problems and ecclesiastical disputes. Rather than establishing simpler procedures and encouraging local solutions to a whole range of administrative and judicial problems, the centralizing trend continued almost uninterrupted during the course of the next several centuries. Along with this development came the need for more and more taxes and assessments of various kinds to support the expanding bureaucracy in the papal court.

Bernard of Clairvaux (1090–1153) warned his former pupil, Pope Eugene III (1145–53), against bringing more and more decisions into the papal curia: "If you love justice, you do not encourage appeals but tolerate them. . . . You do well to refuse judgment on appeals, or rather to refuse protection to them, and return many of these problems to men who are acquainted with them, or who can more quickly become acquainted with them."[25] Bernard also cautioned:

Are you still unaware of what I want to say? I will not keep you in suspense any longer. I speak of the murmuring complaint of the churches. They cry out that they are being mutilated and dismembered. . . . Abbots are freed from the jurisdiction of bishops, bishops from that of archbishops, archbishops from that of patriarchs or primates. Does this seem good? I wonder whether this practice can ever be excused.[26]

Resentment and frustration over the increased taxation and the removal of decision-making authority from the local churches appeared almost everywhere in the West. The pope's curia came to be seen as an endless chain of law courts and administrative offices where privileges and dispensations were made available to simplify and accelerate appointments and decisions of all sorts. The very fabric of the multi-tiered organization of the church, whereby the essentially local and regional character of the organization was realized, became more and more seriously compromised. Even as early as the eleventh century, Archbishop Liemar of Bremen had complained that Pope Gregory VII (1073–85) was reducing the status of the local archbishops and bishops to that of mere bailiffs.[27] The principle of subsidiarity, which affirms that what can be adequately decided at the local level should be decided there, was being seriously compromised, and this began to change the organization of the church in the West.

The practice of holding several parishes at once as well as the practice of not residing at the parish to which one is appointed was strictly forbidden by canon 13 of the Third Lateran Council (1179).[28] However, these two practices—pluralism and non-residence—continued to plague the church for centuries. At Trent nearly four hundred years later, pluralism and non-residence were severely condemned again as extremely damaging to pastoral care.[29] The practice of multiplying offices and benefices considerably enriched the clergy who were the beneficiaries. A good number of curial officials in Rome, for example, had held various pastoral benefices in a number of places in Europe. They would take the lion's share of the revenues themselves, while paying lower clergymen a nominal fee to perform the pastoral duties. This led to abuses and to the notable neglect of the faithful that took centuries to eradicate.

The Albigensians and the Waldensians of southern France, Spain, and northern Italy strenuously opposed the growing wealth of the church, which was alienating the faithful from the authentic values of the gospel. These early reformers were for the most part ordinary people who were convinced that the church had lost its way in the pursuit of riches. With the Cathars in the mid-twelfth century, this reformation became something of a mass movement in southern France, northern Italy, and along the Rhine.[30] A generation later, the Waldensians, who were less radical theologically, were strongly opposed to the sins and abuses of the clergy. The strict moral standards of the Waldensians gained many followers. As their theological positions became more radical, they were attacked by the bishops, labeled as heretics, and hunted down and punished for their allegedly heretical views. These disciples of Peter Waldo advocated a more simple life as reflected in the gospels. Such movements gathered momentum in the twelfth century and constituted a force to be reckoned with by the time of the Fourth Lateran Council in 1215. During the pontificate of Innocent III (1198–1216), the first general tax was levied on the clergy to finance the Fourth Crusade. The abuses of pluralism and absenteeism continued to multiply, as the taxes on the clergy increased the clerical resentment against the papal curia everywhere.

In 1309 the pope moved to Avignon because of the dangerous and unsettled conditions in Italy. The announced objective of the Council of Vienne in 1311 was to address the pressing needs of the church, which were outlined as follows:

1. the weakening of local church government resulting from the growing centralization of power and decision-making in the pope's curia,
2. pluralism and absenteeism,
3. the pope's ever-expanding control over the conferral of more and more offices and parishes in the West, and
4. the mounting burden of taxes levied by the pope on the local churches.

Unfortunately, none of these issues was really addressed at the Council of Vienne, while the Avignon popes continued to be as reckless with their spending as before. The lifestyle of the court during the reign of Clement VI (1342–52) was reportedly the most expensive and luxurious in all of Europe. A group of Franciscans, the Spirituals, grew more and more vocal over the lavish papal lifestyle.

The papal office in the mid-fourteenth century could justly be described as barely spiritual.[31] The English priest John Wyclif (ca. 1330–84), who lived most of his life as a theologian at Oxford, attacked the church because of the pitiable condition of ecclesiastical life and mores in England and the utter confusion generated by the Western Schism. He spoke of the disparity existing between what the church should be versus its actual state. The Western Schism broke out after the death of Pope Gregory XI (1370–78), whose successor, Urban VI (1378–89), was not accepted by the majority of cardinals.

Urban's problem was that he presumed to attack the wealthy lifestyle of the curia. As archbishop of Bari in southern Italy, he was considered an outsider by the curial officials. After it became clear that he intended to wage war against the affluence of the papal court, most of the cardinals left Rome to reside in Anagni, south of the city. Although Urban VI had been harsh and somewhat abusive to the curial people, their real objection was that they did not wish to settle for the simple life that the new pope intended to impose upon them. Hence, they decided to declare the election of Urban VI to be null and void, and the Roman see was declared vacant. The cardinals insisted that Urban had wrongly usurped the papacy. The Anagni contingent then elected a new pope from Geneva, Clement VII (1378–94), claiming that Urban was an evil man who had wrongfully occupied the chair of Peter.

All of Western Christendom was subsequently divided on the issue of the true pope. Urban VI was considered to be the valid claimant in Italy, England, and most of the German countries, while Clement VII was honored as pope by France, Naples, Aragon, and Castile. This intolerable situation was to have been remedied by a new general council held in Pisa in 1409, where the two popes were declared to be notorious schismatics, and a new pope was elected by a group of cardinals who had been attached to one or another of the two claimants, but who strongly felt the need to bring an end to this hopeless impasse. The result was the election of a third pope in 1409, Alexander V, and this further divided the confused and frustrated Christian world. Some dioceses and religious houses were loyal to Urban, others to Clement, and still others to Alexander. This tragic state of affairs that existed throughout the West called for a new general council, which was promoted by King Sigismund of Germany. The council, which opened at Constance in 1414, can justifiably be called the greatest ecclesiastical gathering of the Middle Ages. Two of the papal claimants resigned and the third was deposed, allowing for the election of a new pontiff who would bring all factions together. The conciliar delegates decreed that a general council is the full and supreme expression of the church, having its power immediately from Christ. Moreover, "everyone of whatever state or dignity, even papal, is bound to obey it in those matters which pertain to the faith, the eradication of the said schism and the general reform of the said church of God in head and members."[32] The delegates at Constance later decreed that in the future, general councils were to be held regularly, that is, every ten years. These regular sessions would be a significant help in "cultivating the Lord's patrimony."[33]

Unfortunately, these two conciliar decrees were questioned, debated, and eventually neglected. There is little doubt that, from a human point of view, the general Council of Constance salvaged the papacy, but the tragedy was that the popes after Constance settled back into their monarchical ways and the pressing need for reform was delayed again and again. There is a real possibility that regular general councils after 1415 could have solved many of the abuses that had been infecting and paralyzing the church for centuries, but the opportunity was lost. The tragedy of the Black Death (1447–49), which took 50 percent of the population of Avignon and ran rampant over all of Europe, was not interpreted as a sign of divine disfavor by the papal court, which continued its extravagance. The fifteenth- and early-sixteenth-century Renaissance popes persisted with lavish courts, the selling of offices, and damaging pluralism and absenteeism until they reduced themselves and the papal office to the state of a regional duchy.

Throughout the period there were fervent and repeated cries from all over Christendom for radical reform "in head and members" through the agency of a general council. Some of the principal abuses that needed addressing were set out by a special commission established by Pope Paul III in 1536. The report, issued in 1537, included the following:

1. the accumulation of benefices with the care of souls and the neglect of the obligation of residence,
2. chronic absenteeism on the part of officeholders,
3. the sanctioning of countless cases of simony in the conferral of ecclesiastical offices,
4. the deficient training of the clergy.[34]

Martin Luther's revolt in 1517 radically transformed the ecclesiastical landscape. His message and his charism profoundly affected Europe, especially northern Germany and the Scandinavian countries. The predominant Protestant influence in Switzerland, the Netherlands, France, and Britain was the reformed message of John Calvin (1509–64). After 1560, the Council of Trent (1545–63) had all but given up hope of saving Germany and centered its attention on France, which was gravitating toward Calvinism.

In the Scandinavian countries Lutheranism prevailed, as did Calvinism in the Swiss cantons of Berne, Zurich, Basel, and Geneva; while Lucerne, Fribourg, and Zug remained Catholic. The Netherlands were divided into the Catholic south (Belgium) and the Calvinist north (Holland). In France, Holland, and Scotland, the Protestant movement took on a Calvinistic appearance between 1559 and 1567.[35]

The question of the inevitability of the Protestant Reformation has been widely debated over the years in Catholic circles. Some scholars like Johann Adam Möhler contend that all of the problems precipitating the Reformation would have been corrected over the years from within.[36] There are others, however, who hold that the Reformation was a historical necessity in order to correct the centuries of abuse that were seriously damaging the Christian mission.

> Without the agency of a Martin Luther or someone like him, it is fairly clear that the mind-set of the papacy and the Roman curia was not likely to change. Their financial world was built on pluralism and the fact that they were absent from their lucrative pastoral benefices because of the requirements of the curial posts in Rome. Many of the popes understood the roots of the problem and the underlying corruption of the Roman system for centuries before the revolt of Luther, but even the strongest and the most resolute of them, like Innocent III, were not up to enforcing the necessary changes. . . . The problems of pluralism, non-residence, and excessive taxation to support the Roman bureaucracy had been evident to all for several centuries before the revolt of Luther. Consequently, one finds it rather impossible to affirm with Professor Möhler that things would have corrected themselves in time from within.[37]

Notes

1. William La Due, *The Chair of Saint Peter* (Maryknoll, NY: Orbis, 1999).

2. Hans von Campenhausen, *Ecclesiastical Authority and Spiritual Power in the Church of the First Three Centuries* (trans. J. A. Baker; Stanford: Stanford University Press, 1969), 118.

3. James D. G. Dunn, *Unity and Diversity in the New Testament* (2d ed.; London: SCM, 1990), 122.

4. Karl Baus, *From the Apostolic Community to Constantine* (vol. 1 of *History of the Church*; ed. Hubert Jedin and John Dolan; 1980; repr., Tunbridge Wells: Burns & Oates, 1989), 190–99.

5. *The Treatise on the Apostolic Tradition of St. Hippolytus of Rome* (ed. Gregory Dix and Henry Chadwick; London: Alban Press, reissued 1992), xxvii, xx–xxi, *xxvii.

6. Cyprian, *The Letters of St. Cyprian of Carthage* (trans. G. W. Clarke; vol. 4 of *Ancient Christian Writers* 47; ed. Walter Burghardt and Thomas Lawler; New York: Newman Press, 1989), 54.

7. Ibid., letter 75, 6.1, p. 81.

8. Cyprian, *The Unity of the Catholic Church* (trans. M. Bévenot; vol. 1 of *Ancient Christian Writers* 25; ed. Johannes Quasten and Joseph Plumpe; New York: Newman Press, 1956), chap. 4, p. 46.

9. Giuseppe Alberigo et al., *Decrees of the Ecumenical Councils* (vol. 1; ed. Norman P. Tanner; Washington, DC: Georgetown University Press, 1990), Canon 4, *7. The metropolitan was the bishop who presided in the capital city of the Roman province.

10. Ibid., *85.

11. Walter Ullmann, *A Short History of the Papacy in the Middle Ages* (1972; repr. with additions, New York: Methuen, 1982), 71–72.

12. Thomas F. X. Noble, *The Republic of St. Peter: The Birth of the Papal State, 680–825* (Philadelphia: University of Pennsylvania Press, 1984), 51.

13. Geoffrey Barraclough, *The Medieval Papacy* (New York: Norton, 1968), 40.

14. George Ostrogorsky, *The History of the Byzantine State* (trans. Joan Hussey; 1952; repr., New Brunswick: Rutgers University Press, 1969), 185–86.

15. John Meyendorff, *Imperial Unity and Christian Divisions* (Crestwood, NY: St. Vladimir's Seminary Press, 1989), 327.

16. *Documents of the Christian Church* (3d ed.; ed. Henry Bettenson and Chris Maunder; Oxford: Oxford University Press, 1999), 103.

17. Walter Ullmann, *The Growth of Papal Government in the Middle Ages* (3d ed.; 1955; repr., Northampton: John Dickens & Co., 1970), 209–10.

18. Steven Runciman, *The Eastern Schism* (Oxford: Clarendon Press, 1955), 32.

19. Ibid., 149–50.

20. Ibid.

21. Jaroslav Pelikan, *The Spirit of Eastern Christendom, 600–1700* (vol. 2 of *The Christian Tradition*; Chicago: University of Chicago Press, 1974), 271.

22. Ibid.

23. Runciman, *The Eastern Schism*, 32.

24. Alexander Schmemann, "A Response to the *Decree on Eastern Catholic Churches*," in *The Documents of Vatican II* (ed. Walter M. Abbott; New York: Herder & Herder, 1966), 388.

25. Bernard of Clairvaux, *Five Books on Consideration* (trans. J. Anderson and E. Kennan; Kalamazoo, MI: Cistercian Publications, 1976), 89–93.

26. Ibid., 97–98.

27. Colin Morris, *The Papal Monarchy: The Western Church from 1050–1250* (Oxford: Clarendon Press, 1989), 114.

28. Alberigo et al., *Decrees of the Ecumenical Councils*, 1:*218.

29. Alberigo et al., *Decrees of the Ecumenical Councils*, 2:*770.

30. Hans Wolter, "Heresy and the Beginnings of the Inquisition," in *History of the Church* (vol. 4; ed. Hubert Jedin and John Dolan; New York: Crossroad, 1986), 99.

31. Yves Renouard, *The Avignon Papacy* (trans. D. Bethell; New York: Barnes & Noble, 1970), 116–22.

32. Alberigo et al., *Decrees of the Ecumenical Councils*, 1:*409.

33. Ibid., *438–39.

34. John C. Olin, *Catholic Reform* (New York: Fordham University Press, 1990), 65–79.

35. La Due, *The Chair of Saint Peter*, 202.

36. Joseph Lortz, *How the Reformation Came* (trans. Otto M. Knab; New York: Herder & Herder, 1964), 110–11.

37. La Due, *The Chair of Saint Peter*, 201.

2

THE AGENTS OF THE REFORMATION

Important Developments Preceding the Crisis

No one stream of thought or set of reasons can be credited for the onset of the sixteenth-century Reformation. Most of the decisive developments took place shortly before or shortly after the Council of Constance (1414–18), which has been called one of the most world-shaking events in the religious history of the Middle Ages. From the thirteenth century and the rise of the universities in Europe, there were efforts to reconcile the power and influence of the church with that of the state. In his notable work *On Royal and Papal Power*, John of Paris (ca. 1250–1304) captured the approach of a number of scholars at the University of Paris who maintained that the state and the church are independent entities that have separate power and authority in their respective realms.[1] He contended that there is no radical subordination of the one to the other except in those situations where one entity attempts to assume the role of the other.

Marsilius of Padua (ca. 1275–1342), rector of the University of Padua, wrote an important study, *Defensor Pacis*, in which he insisted that universal ecclesiastical councils are superior to the pope.[2] Marsilius taught that all the clergy from pope to parish priest had roughly the same authority, with the fullness of authority residing in the faithful. The pope receives his power from the faithful, while the faithful manifest their minds most authentically through ecclesiastical councils. The Franciscan scholar William of Ockham (ca. 1300–49) was one of the first to call for an ecumenical council to address the growing crisis fermenting in the church.[3]

Pierre D'Ailly (1350–1420), a theologian at the University of Paris, held that the pope is in fact a constitutional monarch whose authority is limited, and that the full realization of ecclesiastical power rests in the universal ecumenical council.[4] A student of D'Ailly at Paris, Jean Gerson (1363–1423), reflecting on the situation of the church during the Western Schism (1378–1417), insisted that a universal council was above the pope. Both council and pope share the highest authority, but the council constitutes the prevailing authority.[5] Much of this thinking was deeply influenced by the tragic circumstances of the time. After 1378, there were two papal claimants, and after 1409, there were three. Each had his dedicated followers who were convinced that the other claimants were either heretics or schismatics. Throughout all of Christendom, dioceses, parishes, and religious institutions of all kinds were deeply divided—one expressing allegiance to a particular claimant and accusing the other or others of precipitating schism. The only conceivable solution could be found in a universal council, inasmuch as the church was literally being torn apart, and there was no other viable alternative.

Out of this seemingly hopeless situation, the conciliar movement came into prominence. Although it was given its form by scholars, it was grounded in the actual distress of the Western Schism, which none of the three papal claimants had any power to heal. An impasse of these dimensions was clearly beyond the power of any pope to address effectively. This real-life situation opened a new direction in constitutional thought for the church. For centuries, the papacy was the usual, the normal, the supreme authority within the church, and the last resort for the solution of governmental crises within the church. However, in the event of a situation like the Western Schism, there had to be another human authority that, in an emergency like this one, could be called upon as the controlling agent. If the pope was in manifest heresy or was destroying the fabric of the church and its mission, there had to be a higher authority that could intervene to steer the wavering ship back on course. The council was not considered a permanent and ordinary ruling body, but in crises of grave emergency, it was considered by the moderate conciliarists to have the responsibility and the authority to intervene and address what was otherwise a desperate situation. This mindset constituted the point of departure for what has come to be called the conciliar movement. The so-called *via concilii* seemed to be the only way to address the stalemate caused by the three rival popes, each of whom claimed to be the true and sole successor of Peter.

The Council of Constance opened on November 16, 1414, with the awesome mission of healing the deep fractures in the church. John XXIII, the papal claimant of the Pisan line, opened the first session, which was to promote the peace and reform of the church and to quiet the hearts of the Christian people.[6] On April 6, 1415, the council declared that its power was immediately from Christ and that everyone, even the papacy itself, was to obey those enactments "which pertain to the faith, the eradication of the said schism, and the general reform of the said church of God in head and members."[7] This much-debated decree (*Haec sancta synodus*) declared in no uncertain terms that the general council has the supreme authority in the church regarding the elimination of schism and the general reform of the church. "The council simply had to assume the sovereign power over the three claimants in order to break the deadlock. In this, and presumably in any similar situation, the council was the body that represented the universal church which needed and demanded a solution to the impasse."[8]

Although a number of scholars have refused to see any permanent validity in this conciliar principle (e.g., Joseph Gill), others are convinced that it does establish a new constitutional precedent (e.g., Brian Tierney). In spite of the fact that the fullness of governing power resides in the pope, in another sense, this full sovereignty rests in the universal church and in a universal council that represents it when there is no possible agreement regarding the true pope. There is in effect what Brian Tierney has termed a "divided sovereignty," which in such a circumstance is shared by both the papacy and the universal church gathered together in an ecumenical council.[9] Furthermore, in October 1417, the Council of Constance enacted a schedule for the regular convocation of general councils in the future: "We establish, enact, decree and ordain, by a perpetual edict, that general councils shall be held hereafter in the following way. The first shall follow in five years immediately after the end of this council, the second in seven years immediately after the end of the next council, and thereafter they are to be held every ten years forever."[10]

After the mixed results of the Council of Basel-Ferrara-Florence (1431–45), and in spite of the self-defeating efforts of the extreme wing of the conciliarists in the mid-1430s and the 1440s, in the fifteenth and sixteenth centuries there were consistent and repeated cries all over Christendom for a universal council to correct the manifold abuses in head and members. There was a deep and abiding conviction held by many bishops and laity alike that only through the instrumentality of a general council could the widespread ills paralyzing the church and its mission be effectively addressed. Almost every pontificate from Martin V (1417–31) to Paul III (1534–49) had to listen to the resounding petitions throughout Christendom for a reform council to heal the church in head and members. The strong hand that the popes wielded during the Council of Trent (1545–63) in orchestrating the agenda and the discourse seemed to deaden the continuing appeals for reform through the agency of universal councils. In fact, another ecumenical council was not convoked until 1869 (Vatican I). The one attempt to broaden the governing base of the Catholic Church growing out of the Council of Constance (1414–18) seemed to have lost its way until Vatican II (1962–65) and its articulation of the principle of collegiality—which has never been seriously implemented in the past forty years after Vatican II. The governance of the Catholic Church continues to follow the contours of the absolutist model refined at Vatican I and expanded by the popes from 1870 to the present.

This concludes a brief account of the efforts of the moderate conciliarists and their followers to broaden the political base of Catholicism. We shall see that while most other Christian denominations in the West have moved toward more representative ecclesial structures based on the principal of the priesthood of all believers, the Catholic Church has remained largely a top-down organization, grounded in the Petrine prerogatives alluded to in Matthew 16. Peter's prerogatives, however, as reflected in the rest of the New Testament, do not seem to assign him the sweeping, monarchical role that the papacy has acquired, especially in the last two hundred years. Catholic theologians in the second part of this work will address the issue of papal government in greater detail.

Martin Luther (1483–1546)

In his *Ninety-Five Theses* published in October 1517, Martin Luther openly criticized the practice of indulgences current in his day. His principal complaints revolved around the use of authority in the Catholic Church.[11] He thus took pains to provide a direction for the Reformation church, desiring to preserve the episcopal hierarchy, but in this he was only partially successful. Martin saw himself as the one prompted by God to undertake the reforms he set out to achieve.[12] The period from 1514 to 1518, while he was teaching theology at Wittenberg, allowed him to formulate his vigorous program of reform. After he was excommunicated by church authorities in January 1521, Luther's criticism of the papacy became more and more strident.

Luther's concentration on the unassailable authority of the words of sacred Scripture was unprecedented. For him, the biblical word and "clear reason" were the ultimate criteria of Christian truth. He did not especially concentrate on the theology of church. Luther wanted to keep the church's episcopal structure because he was convinced that the preaching of the gospel and the guidance of pastors were principally episcopal prerogatives. The bishops and their synods represented for him a necessary framework for the church. He believed that the parishes are to create order as required so that the preaching of the Word, worship, and the life of communities can be sustained and promoted.[13] He desired that bishops be chosen and installed by prominent members of the larger community. That function, however, was soon taken over by the German territorial princes. To avoid endless confusion, Luther said that preaching must not be performed by all believers. Thus, congregations are to call ministers to perform the function on behalf of all.[14] In this instance, Luther emphasized the power of the office over the priesthood of all believers.

Although the *Augsburg Confession* was composed by Philip Melanchthon for the Diet of Augsburg in 1530 because Luther had been forbidden by ecclesiastical authority to attend, it does set forth distinctly the basic Lutheran positions. In fact, it became the most influential of all the Lutheran creeds.[15] Article IV of the *Augsburg Confession* asserts that it is through faith and the grace of faith that we become righteous. Christ suffered for us and, because of him, our sins are forgiven, righteousness and eternal life are given to us.[16] God considers this faith of ours as righteousness. Through the office of the ministry, this faith is proclaimed and makes available to us the gospel and the sacraments.

The Christian church—which will remain forever—is defined as the assembly of all believers to whom the true gospel is preached and the sacraments are rightly administered.[17] In Article IX of the *Augsburg Confession*, baptism is declared to be necessary and is to be conferred on children.[18] The Lord's Supper renders present the true body and blood of Christ (Article X), and private absolution is to be retained, although it is never necessary to enumerate each and every sin committed, because this is frequently not possible (Article XI). The mass is described not as a sacrifice, but as a communion wherein those in attendance receive the body and blood of the Lord (Article XXIV). In Article XXVIII, the office of the bishop is identified in terms of the obligation to preach the gospel, to forgive sins, to judge and condemn doctrine contrary to the gospel, and to exclude the ungodly from the Christian community.[19] The *Augsburg Confession* concludes with the observation that the grave complaints regarding indulgences have been omitted in order that the crucial issues under discussion can be more fully appreciated.[20]

In 1537, Luther composed *The Schmalkald Articles*, which summarized what he considered his own mature theological perspective. In this work, which was written after Paul III's proclamation of a general council in 1536, Martin was making a definitive theological statement prior to his death.[21] In Article 2, he affirms that we are not obliged to attend mass under pain of grievous sin and insists that such things as relics are useless items. He also opposes prayers and supplications to the saints as a Christian abuse. Martin asserts that Augustine had not written about the existence of purgatory, thus leaving this matter undecided.[22]

In Article 4, the authority of the pope is restricted entirely to the church at Rome, for he is not a necessary figure in the whole church. Actually, if there is to be a single leader of Christendom, that person should be elected by all the faithful, and he should remain in power at the discretion of the faithful.[23] Should a leader of this sort be chosen, he need not reside in Rome. There is indeed one ruler of the whole church, and that is Christ. All bishops wherever stationed are of equal rank, maintaining the one true doctrine, the sacraments, and prayers.[24] Because the pope has elevated himself over all other bishops, he reveals in effect that he is the antichrist.

In the article on the law, Luther insisted that the precise enumeration of one's sins in confession is often impossible because one could never know whether or not the confession was complete. He did warn, however, that confession and absolution should not be allowed to fall into disuse.[25] Regarding the presence of Christ in the Eucharist, Martin held that the bread and wine truly contain the body and blood of the Lord. However, he considered the Catholic thesis of transubstantiation to be false.[26] The ordination of worthy ministers should be one of the primary roles of bishops, but all the ceremonial pomp and pretense must be set aside. In one of his final observations, Luther stressed that priests should be allowed to marry because marriage must be free, as God ordained it. Nor did he allow for such things as the blessing and consecration of churches, bells, and altar stones—all of which he considered pointless.[27]

Martin Luther defined the church as a communion of saints, a community gathered around the Word of God and the sacraments of baptism and the Lord's Supper. The church is apostolic because it feeds on the apostolic gospel and therefore represents the true apostolic succession. The church is both visible and invisible and is related to the church in heaven and the church suffering in purgatory.[28] There can be no transfer of merits from one person to another, for this arrangement has lost all meaning. Christ covers over our sins and intercedes for us with his righteousness.[29] Luther was opposed to the rule requiring annual confession, which he viewed as a priestly service that one could simply request from a brother or a friend.

Although all Christians receive the priesthood from Christ, the community must call individuals to fulfill the office of public ministry. For Luther, the office of preaching is the most noble office in the church. Ordination is simply the call to carry out the office of ministry, and it involves the reading of appropriate passages from sacred Scripture, recitation of prayers, and the laying on of hands.[30] For Luther, Scripture is the standard for judging church tradition, determining whether it is true and correct. It must be affirmed that the Holy Spirit continually guides the believing community, just as the Spirit did in the apostolic church.[31] It can indeed occur in certain situations that we must disobey the church in order that we might obey Christ and his Word.

Luther taught that the legitimacy of a church council depends entirely on the apostolicity of its doctrine. Nor does the apostolic succession of bishops necessarily guarantee the apostolic succession of truth.

> According to the theology of the resurrection God has always preserved his church, even under a church organization such as the papacy which erred in many ways. He has done this by marvelously preserving the text of the gospel and the sacraments; and through these many have lived and died in true faith. This remains true even though they were only a weak and hidden minority within the official church. Luther repeatedly says this.[32]

The Lutheran theologian Paul Althaus concludes his chapter, "The True Church and the Empirical Church," as follows:

> Luther, as we have seen, points out, that in a specific situation in the church, one single individual might have the truth; he then must constantly maintain it against the authorities of the official church. . . . God allows the official church to err in order to destroy the ever present danger that men trust in the church rather than in God's word alone. Then, however, God again sends the church witnesses to his truth.[33]

Luther's work *On the Councils of the Church* (1539) constituted the beginning of what could be called a Protestant theology of church authority.[34] Jaroslav Pelikan has this to say regarding Luther's approach to church structures:

> Luther's indifference to the traditional issues of church structure, which to his critics on many sides seemed cavalier, helped to make it possible for his followers to accommodate themselves to systems of ecclesiastical organization ranging from state church to free church and from a retention of the historic episcopate to (at least theoretical) congregationalism, with doctrine rather than polity as the decisive principle separating them from all others.[35]

According to Erwin Iserloh, Luther did not offer a detailed theology of the church: Wherever the authentic gospel is proclaimed and the sacraments are rightly administered, the true church lives in the external church.[36] Luther did, however, insist that some sort of organization must exist above the local level to insure church order and some uniformity from place to place. He expected that each individual congregation would create a workable organization and bring forth the institutions necessary for worship and for a healthy community life. He felt that if the current bishops within the papal system were not appropriate for the call to office, then the leading members of each congregation should replace them with other suitable leaders.[37] As the territorial lords began to assume the role of selecting bishops, Luther gave less and less thought to questions of church order. Furthermore, he was convinced that he was living in the last days, and this colored his approach to organizational details.

However, in Germany in the mid-sixteenth century, there was no little confusion about doctrine, since the *Confessio Augustana* (i.e., the *Confession of Augsburg*) was not adequate to stem the rising tide of doctrinal controversy among the followers of Luther. Some fifty years after the *Confessio Augustana*, the *Book of Concord* was published (1580) to achieve a greater degree of doctrinal unity. Nevertheless, the situation still remained rather unsettled.

> Denominational uncertainty, frequent change, and the circumstance that pastors suitable for the religion decreed from above were not available fostered indifference and increased the number of those who no longer went at all to the church and the Sacraments. . . . Crass ignorance in matters of faith, neglect of religion, and immorality characterized the situation in the second half of the sixteenth century cutting across all denominations.[38]

Luther was convinced that the German territorial princes should take an active part in the reorganization of the church. He felt that this responsibility flowed out of the doctrine of the priesthood of all the faithful. The princes in turn assumed the former jurisdiction of the bishops through the appointment of consistories.

> The consistory, the characteristic agent of church government in Lutheran (as later in Reformed) churches, was not created at once in every Lutheran state. . . . The consistory was normally composed of lawyers and divines, and appointed by the prince. It was regarded rather as a Church court than a civil court, though the distinction has less meaning than it would have a century later. . . . The consistory exercised all discipline.[39]

As the sixteenth century unfolded, superintendents were instituted to replace the office of bishops. By the time of the Peace of Westphalia (1648), the church territories in northern Germany were no longer in Catholic control.[40] The west and the south of Germany, along with Austria and Hungary, remained largely Catholic. However, the north and the east would stay Lutheran, along with the Scandinavian countries.

John Calvin (1509–64)

John Calvin was very different in temperament, background, and theological orientation from Martin Luther. By no means is his thinking easy to understand. While Luther was very open and expressive, Calvin was more reserved and withdrawn.[41] In his favorite New Testament book, 2 Timothy, Calvin could see himself as the elder Paul dispensing pastoral advice to his young followers as Paul did to Timothy. Heiko Oberman points to the dogmas of election and predestination as perhaps the major limitations of Calvinism.[42] The notion of double predestination has been viewed by many over the years as a significant drawback and an invitation to fatalism.[43] In spite of this, Calvinism proved to be extremely popular and became well established in the Netherlands, Scotland, and the United States. For Calvin, the Christian church was primarily a local community, but he was not especially fond of Luther's priesthood of all believers. Calvin was dedicated to a more authoritarian pattern of control.[44]

He believed that the clergy are to command. There is to be the office of pastor and a senate of elders in each congregation. The function of the pastor is to proclaim the Word, administer the sacraments, exhort, and censure those who are wayward. Further, pastors are to be elected by all the members of the congregation. For Calvin, the clergy are to be in control, while laypersons are to oversee the conduct of all church members. A sufficient number of these officials are necessary to watch over all aspects of the life of the congregation and to admonish those who require correction. Each congregation is to have a senate of mature and holy men called elders who possess specific jurisdiction over the correcting of faults. Calvin also ordered that there be doctors selected to lecture the various congregations on the Old and New Testaments and on true doctrine. These men are to be trained in the biblical texts and be capable of instructing the members of the church, both young and old. Finally, a number of deacons are to be appointed in each congregation to care for the poor and the needy. John Calvin's *Ecclesiastical Ordinances* of 1541 laid out this plan for the city of Geneva, and a similar format was followed in most of his congregations.[45] In his *Institutes of the Christian Religion*, first published in 1536 and revised several times until the final edition in 1559, Calvin outlined his basic theology, along with a detailed pattern of church order for his congregations. Over the years, the work grew from six to eighty chapters. In book 4, "The Nature and Function of the Church," Calvin assures his followers that as long as believers remain within the bosom of the church, the truth will always abide with them.[46] Furthermore, for those falling away from the body of the church, there will be no forgiveness of sin or any salvation. The visible church exists where the Word of God is purely preached and heard and the sacraments are administered according to Christ's institution. These, for Calvin, are the first two discernible marks of the church of Christ. If one cuts himself or herself off from the communion of the visible church, he or she is removed from the communion of saints.[47]

Calvin taught that Christ promised his mercy solely within the communion of saints, where our sins are pardoned daily as long as we remain grafted into the body of the church.[48] According to Calvin, those who assume public office in the church must be duly called and approved by the people. Other pastors in the vicinity must preside over the election of new pastors so that the appropriate candidates are selected. Those who are chosen must be of sound doctrine and manifest a holy life. In the ordination ceremony, the laying on of hands may be used.

John Calvin took very seriously the need to give detailed directions for the organization and management of the parishes. He insisted that his ministers not devise or confect any new doctrines outside of what is contained in the Scriptures. The Law, the Prophets, and the Historical Books constitute the Lord's Word for the Old Testament people, and the writings of the apostles are the only authorized sources of Christ's teaching in the church.[49] According to Calvin, organization is indispensable for any human society in order to promote the common peace. Laws are also essential. However, only those ordinances that are grounded in Scripture are acceptable. The directives that are not necessary for salvation and for the edification of the church can be adapted and changed according to the customs of each nation and each age.[50] In addition to the authentic preaching of the gospel and the administration of the sacraments according to the institution of Christ, the third and final mark of the church is discipline, which the various laws and regulations outlined above should provide.

In France, the Protestants, or Huguenots, were allowed to meet publicly during Henry IV's reign (1589–1610). However, after 1685, approximately four hundred thousand Huguenots were driven from France into the Low Countries, Germany, the New World, and elsewhere. In the Netherlands, the Reformed church, organized into local consistories and regional gatherings, was flourishing in the seventeenth century. Calvinism in Scotland grew strong, especially under the leadership of John Knox (1514–72), who adopted Calvin's thought in the 1550s. According to the Scottish Confession of 1560, candidates for the ministry are to be elected by the people. In seventeenth-century Scotland, bishops became obsolete and were replaced by superintendents whose role it was to oversee and maintain discipline. After 1550 or thereabouts, Calvinism appeared in England, and predestination was interpreted in conformity with the *Thirty-Nine Articles* of the Church of England, which reached their final form in 1571. The Calvinists desired a presbyterian structure (thus eliminating the bishops), but that was realized for only a brief period from 1643 to the reign of Charles II (1660–85).

The English Reformation

The English Reformation had its roots in the fourteenth century with protests against papalism, along with the rising tide of anticlericalism. John Wyclif (1320–84), an Oxford scholar, was a strategic voice in the protests against the venality and ignorance of the English clergy of his day. He was instrumental in generating a flood of dissent among the wealthy as well as the poor. The Lollards took up the cry for reform and carried it into the sixteenth century. With Henry VIII (1509–47), the country was ripe for religious revolt. Henry's battle against Pope Clement VII (1523–34) over his failed marriage to Catherine of Aragon proved unsuccessful, and the king responded with the Act of Supremacy (1534), in which Henry severed England's relationship with Rome. Henry declared himself head of the Church of England after Cardinal Wolsey was unable to obtain a papal annulment for him. Under Edward VI (1547–53), who was nine years old at his accession, the nation gravitated toward Calvinism under the leadership of Thomas Cranmer (1489–1556), who was appointed Archbishop of Canterbury in 1532. Cranmer was the principal author of the liturgical and doctrinal reforms of the English church.[51] The confiscation of ecclesiastical property and the dissolution of monasteries followed the breach with Rome. According to Owen Chadwick:

> Everyone is agreed that in all countries of Europe the Church, as a collection of corporations, possessed too much wealth for the health of the state, that some diversion was necessary, and that material transfers of property are always painful and usually accompanied by injustice to individuals. . . . The gravamen is not that the Church suffered a crippling loss of endowment, but that the Protestant sovereigns of Europe, in their need for money, missed a unique opportunity of converting these charitable resources to truly charitable ends like education, hospitals, or the relief of the poor. It would be not so severe a charge if it

could be shown that the endowments were diverted to truly national ends.[52]

During Edward's reign (1547–53), the clergy were permitted to marry, and communion under both kinds was initiated. The second *Book of Common Prayer* was issued in 1552, and Cranmer published his *Forty-Two Articles* in 1553. Under Queen Mary (1552–58), relations with Rome were restored and many Catholic monasteries were reopened. Since Mary had no heir, she was succeeded by her sister Elizabeth, who reigned for forty-five years (1558–1603). The resumption of the Act of Supremacy in 1559 ended papal jurisdiction in England once and for all. In 1563, the *Thirty-Nine Articles*—a revision of the *Forty-Two Articles*—were promulgated: "The Articles are not as comprehensive as many of the Continental creeds. Neither do they have the full authority that was given to the creeds in Lutheran and Reformed churches. They are moderate in theological expression and are designed to provide a minimal basis for a comprehensive, national church that sought to preserve both the Catholic and Protestant traditions."[53]

The *Thirty-Nine Articles* provided the foundation of Christian belief among the Anglicans. The episcopal structure, which was preserved, offered the continuity between the new and the old. The Bible was declared to be the supreme rule of faith, along with the first four general councils. Thus, the Church of England remained in basic agreement with the mainline Protestants on the Continent. The definition of the church was stated in roughly the same terms as in the Lutheran and Reformed bodies: "The visible Church of Christ is a congregation of faithful men, in which the pure Word of God is preached, and the Sacraments are duly ministered according to Christ's ordinance, and all those things that of necessity are requisite to the same."[54] Purgatory was eliminated, as was the veneration of relics. Overall, there was considerable flexibility in what the faithful were asked to believe. In addition, Cranmer's *Book of Common Prayer* was acknowledged as the standard liturgical text.

The seventeenth century saw two discernible camps in the Church of England, the Puritans and the Episcopalians.[55] The *Westminster Confession* (1646), which was composed during the Puritan revolution, "represents the precision and comprehensiveness of a fully developed theology."[56] The Confession became the standard creed of the Presbyterians. Under the Puritans, the *Book of Common Prayer* was banned, and no provision was made for the role of bishops. However, with Charles II (1660–85), the *Book of Common Prayer* was restored along with the episcopal order.

John Wesley (1703–91) and Methodism

The late seventeenth and early eighteenth centuries witnessed the rise of rationalism, which had a profound effect on the Christian churches. Pietism in Holland, Germany, and England rather dramatically deemphasized the scientific study of theology and focused on the cult of the *praxis pietatis*, the practice of piety, which can be described as "faith demonstrated in the life of each individual as well as in the life of the church."[57] Emphasis was placed on feelings, and religion was seen as a revival of the emotional dimensions of faith.

John Wesley, who was influenced as a youth by the Pietist movement, embarked during his Oxford years upon a search for perfection involving a fixed daily order consisting of prayer, reading, and mortification.[58] His methodical approach to the pursuit of perfection prompted others to call him and his disciples Methodists. After an unsuccessful journey to the colony of Georgia in America, Wesley returned to London and began an energetic preaching career. He and his younger brother, Charles the hymnist (1707–88), traveled the length and breadth of England. Not many congregations opened their doors to John, so he preached wherever he could, even in the open countryside. His goal was to produce "the felt experience of being loved and forgiven by God."[59] The Wesleys touched the hearts of thousands with their message and their songs. John remained an Anglican throughout his entire life. His thoughts regarding church order were rather simple. The laity and the ministry are to have equal but distinct functions in the church. The Wesleys were not apostles of social change but dedicated themselves to bringing the warmth of religion to many.[60]

John Wesley revised the *Thirty-Nine Articles* of the Church of England and formulated his *Twenty-Five Articles of Religion*, which were ratified by the Methodist conference in Baltimore in 1784.[61] He defines the church as "the visible church of Christ, a congregation of faithful men in which the pure Word of God is preached and the sacraments duly administered, according to Christ's ordinances, in all those things that of necessity are requisite to the same."[62] According to Wesley, there are two sacraments, baptism and the Lord's Supper. The body of Christ in communion is taken in a heavenly and spiritual manner. The rites and ceremonies of worship can be diverse in accordance with the customs of various times and places. "Every particular Church may ordain, change, or abolish rites and ceremonies, so that all things may be done to edification." Further, "the ministers of Christ are not commanded by God's law either to vow the estate of single life or to abstain from marriage. . . ."[63] Wesley felt strongly that the Anglican Church of his day had drifted away from the Scriptures, and it was his mission to revive and restore a deeper biblical orientation. He continually aimed at the practice of Christian perfection for all believers, and his own thoughts on church organization did not vary greatly from the arrangements in the Church of England in the eighteenth century. However, John Wesley's singular emphasis was on teaching, preaching circuits, and general conferences. His message continues to be efficacious in many parts of the world.

John Wesley has been called the most important theologian in the Anglican evangelical tradition.[64] He left the academic life at Oxford to engage in the "street work" of the evangelical revival.[65] He preached to the ordinary, the poor, and the laborers to bring them the gospel of Jesus and to instill in them the piety and eager spirit that animated his lifelong mission. His folk theology expressed itself in simple liturgies. Although a Calvinist in many ways, he was opposed to the doctrine of predestination because it attacked the divine goodness. "Wesley's ministry was irregular. . . . His doctrine was denounced as 'enthusiasm'; his discipline was deplored as fanaticism." Wesley took the gospel seriously and relied on God's promise of full salvation "with a lively expectation."[66]

The Baptists

The origin of the Baptists is usually traced back to the Puritan and Separatist movements of the seventeenth century. The Separatists believed churches should include only those who are consciously and actively Christian. Each congregation is to be self-governing, and no church is to have authority over any other church. The Separatists were the spiritual predecessors of the Congregationalists. Some are convinced that the Baptist movement really originated on the banks of the Jordan River with John the Baptist. Until recent times, there was little effort to construct a Baptist theology of church. In his *Systematic Theology*, published in 1907, the Baptist theologian Augustus Hopkins Strong defined the universal church as "the whole company of regenerate persons of all times and all ages," and the local church as "that in which the universal church takes local and temporal form."[67] The Baptists generally believe that the church is only comprised of regenerate persons, that is, those who firmly believe and have freely submitted to baptism as adults. The visible church can be more fully described as the aggregate of faithful and penitent persons baptized by immersion, separated out of the world, walking together in communion.[68] The local congregations are to possess the power to receive and exclude members, as well as the power to elect and preside over the ordination of their own ministers.

Their insistence on believers' baptism by immersion and their conviction that baptism be available only to those who personally profess the faith constitute indispensable tenets of the Baptist position. The reception of baptism does not really cause spiritual regeneration but symbolizes it, because the subject is already regenerated through his adult faith and repentance.[69] Each member is considered to have an equal voice in the decision-making of the local church, which encourages the members to promote democratic ideals in the other dimensions of their lives. In spite of possible varieties in church discipline from congregation to congregation, all Baptists are uniformly opposed to the practice of infant baptism.

Strong asserts that the form of church polity is not specified in the New Testament, "but is a matter of expediency, each body of believers being permitted to adopt that method of organization which best suits its circumstances and condition."[70] There is no jurisdiction or control of one church over another, for all are on an equal footing. Each local church is to promote the glory of God through prayer, religious instruction, mutual concern, and by laboring to reclaim the sinful world.[71]

Although Christ is the primary lawgiver for the church, it is the role of the entire organization to maintain pure doctrine and practice. The church can be considered both democratic and congregational.[72] There is abundant evidence that a hierarchical form of church governance corrupts the church and has no clear advantage over the congregational form of polity.[73] Strong asserts that there are two offices in the church—that of bishop or presbyter or pastor, and that of deacon. The office of bishop or presbyter is the same, and the term pastor simply indicates the specific role of the individual. Another name for presbyter in the Baptist nomenclature is elder. The role of the presbyter is to be the teacher, the administrator, the supervisor of discipline, and the presiding officer at meetings. The deacon, on the other hand, is an assistant or helper for the pastor and the church.

Ordination as described by Strong does not involve the conferral of powers but is simply a recognition of one's own talents and abilities plus an authorization by the church to exercise the gifts already possessed.[74] Although the power of ordination rests with the local church, other nearby churches are requested to give their formal permission, which would enable the one who is ordained to exercise his ministry within the jurisdiction of such churches. The various local churches are to have a relationship of fellowship among equals, and they are to consult one another regarding issues of common interest.[75]

In spite of the fact that in Baptist theology there has been relatively little thought given to the notion of the universal church, there has always been a persistent passion for the rights and prerogatives of the individual.[76] The organizational structure above the local church has looked to a local association of congregations, the state and national conventions, and ultimately to the Baptist World Alliance.[77] However, the Baptists always give a clear priority to the individual and to the local church as an independent entity among equals. The missionary role of Baptist congregations, especially regarding the need to act as a leaven to transform the current culture and to Christianize it, has been set out with a broad vision by James Wm. McClendon Jr. in the third volume of his *Systematic Theology*, published in 2000.[78]

This overview has been an attempt to revisit the notions of church of the major Reformation bodies from the sixteenth century to 1800 as a preface to our review of a group of theologians who have contributed in a significant manner to the development of our current understanding of church. Other theologians could have been selected, but these are the ones that have contributed most—in my judgment—to the expansion of the contemporary understanding of the complicated reality that is the Christian church or, perhaps more correctly, the Christian churches.

Notes

1. John of Paris, *On Royal and Papal Power* (trans. J. A. Watt; Toronto: Pontifical Institute of Mediaeval Studies, 1971).

2. Marsilius of Padua, *Defensor Pacis* (trans. Alan Gewirth; Toronto: University of Toronto Press, 1980).

3. Frederick Copleston, *A History of Philosophy* (vol. 3; Garden City, NY: Image Books, 1952), 120–21.

4. Steven Ozment, *The Age of Reform 1250–1550* (New Haven: Yale University Press, 1980), 171.

5. Ibid., 170, 179.

6. Giuseppe Alberigo et al., *Decrees of the Ecumenical Councils* (vol. 1; ed. Norman P. Tanner; Washington, DC: Georgetown University Press, 1990), *405.

7. Ibid., *409.

8. William La Due, *The Chair of Saint Peter* (Maryknoll, NY: Orbis, 1999), 162.

9. Brian Tierney, "Divided Sovereignty at Constance: A Problem of Medieval and Early Modern Political Theory," repr. in *Church Law and Constitutional Thought in the Middle Ages* (London: Variorum Reprints, 1979), 244.

10. Alberigo et al., *Decrees of the Ecumenical Councils* 1:*439.

11. Bernhard Lohse, *Martin Luther: An Introduction to His Life and Work* (trans. Robert C. Schultz; Philadelphia: Fortress, 1986), 48.

12. Ibid., 91.

13. Erwin Iserloh, "The Reform in the German Principalities," in *History of the Church* (vol. 5; ed. Hubert Jedin and John Dolan; New York: Crossroad, 1990), 221.

14. Ibid., 215.

15. *Creeds of the Churches* (3d ed.; ed. John H. Leith; Louisville, KY: John Knox, 1982), 64.

16. Ibid., 69.

17. Ibid., 70.

18. Ibid.

19. Ibid., 97–99.

20. Ibid., 106.

21. Martin Luther, *The Schmalkald Articles* (trans. William R. Russell; Minneapolis: Fortress, 1955), vii.

22. Ibid., 7–11.

23. Ibid., 6–7.

24. Ibid., 8–10.

25. Ibid., 21–22.

26. Ibid., 27–28. While denying the doctrine of transubstantiation, Luther consistently held to the concept of consubstantiation, although it is doubtful whether he ever used the term. Consubstantiation means that Christ is bodily present in and with the elements of bread and wine, which are not essentially changed.

27. Ibid., 31–33.

28. Paul Althaus, *The Theology of Martin Luther* (trans. Robert C. Schultz; Philadelphia: Fortress, 1966), 292.

29. Ibid., 310.

30. Ibid., 332.

31. Ibid., 338–39.

32. Ibid., 343.

33. Ibid., 344.

34. B. A. Gerrish, *Continuing the Reformation* (Chicago: University of Chicago Press, 1993), 51.

35. Jaroslav Pelikan, *Reformation of Church and Dogma (1300–1700)* (vol. 4 of *The Christian Tradition*; Chicago: University of Chicago Press, 1984), 313.

36. Iserloh, "The Reform in the German Principalities," 213–14.

37. Ibid., 221.

38. Ibid., 424.

39. Owen Chadwick, *The Reformation* (1964; repr., New York: Viking Penguin, 1986), 69.

40. Kurt Aland, *A History of Christianity* (vol. 2; trans. James L. Schaaf; Philadelphia: Fortress, 1986), 217.

41. Heiko Oberman, *The Two Reformations* (ed. Donald Weinstein; New Haven: Yale University Press, 2003), 126.

42. Ibid., 147.

43. Double predestination can be described as follows: Some from the beginning of their lives are irrevocably destined for hell, while others are similarly destined for salvation.

44. William Bouwsma, *John Calvin: A Sixteenth-Century Portrait* (New York: Oxford University Press, 1988), 219.

45. Lewis Spitz, ed. *The Protestant Reformation, 1517–1559* (New York: Harper & Row, 1985), 122–29.

46. *Calvin's Institutes: A New Compend* (ed. Hugh T. Kerr; Louisville, KY: Westminster/John Knox, 1989), 130.

47. Ibid., 135.

48. Ibid., 136.

49. Ibid., 145–46.

50. Ibid., 150.

51. William A. Scott, *Historical Protestantism: An Historical Introduction to Protestant Theology* (Englewood Cliffs, NJ: Prentice-Hall, 1971), 70.

52. Chadwick, *The Reformation*, 109.

53. *Creeds of the Churches*, ed. Leith, 266.

54. Ibid., 273.

55. Chadwick, *The Reformation*, 230.

56. *Creeds of the Churches*, ed. Leith, 192.

57. Aland, *History of Christianity*, 235–36.

58. Scott, *A Historical Protestantism*, 98.

59. Ibid., 100.

60. Ibid., 108.

61. *Creeds of the Churches*, ed. Leith, 353.

62. Ibid., 357.

63. Ibid., 359–60.

64. Albert Outler, *The Wesleyan Theological Heritage: Essays of Albert C. Outler* (introduced and ed. Thomas Oden and Leicester Longden; Grand Rapids, MI: Zondervan, 1991), 12.

65. Ibid., 13.

66. Ibid., 47–49.

67. Augustus Hopkins Strong, *Systematic Theology: A Compendium* (Valley Forge, PA: Judson, 1907), 887, 889.

68. E. Jeffrey Mask, *At Liberty under God: Toward a Baptist Ecclesiology* (Lanham, MD: University Press of America, 1997), 50.

69. Ibid., 60.

70. Strong, *Systematic Theology*, 896.

71. Ibid., 899.

72. Ibid., 904.

73. Ibid., 912.

74. Ibid., 918.

75. Ibid., 927.

76. Mask, *At Liberty under God*, 104.

77. Ibid., 172.

78. James Wm. McClendon Jr., *Witness: Systematic Theology* (vol. 3; Nashville, TN: Abingdon Press, 2000), 345–420.

3

PROTESTANT ECCLESIOLOGY COMES OF AGE

Friedrich Schleiermacher (1768–1834)

Largely because of his Moravian upbringing, Friedrich Schleiermacher was extremely sensitive to the significance of religious feeling, which colored his doctrinal stance in many ways. Called by some the father of liberal theology, he taught at the universities of Halle and Berlin. Schleiermacher consistently gave strong support for a union between the Lutheran and Reformed traditions. *The Christian Faith*, his major theological work, which was first published in 1821–22 and revised in 1830, found him quoting Lutheran confessions and scholars more frequently than Reformed sources.[1] He truly intended that *The Christian Faith* be received as a dogmatic treatise of the united churches in Germany. He remained firm in his conviction that there were no essential differences between the two communions.

In 1799, he published a short piece, *On Religion: Speeches to Its Cultured Despisers*, to explain his views on religion. It was directed to his circle of friends, like Friedrich von Schlegel, who were attracted by the ideas of natural religion and the Romantic movement. Schleiermacher is opposed to the notion that formal religious association inevitably leads to discord and dissension.[2] He favors dialogue as the way to foster true religious experience. Addressing the form in which the church should appeal to the world, he vigorously opposes any union between the church and the state as destructive to religion.[3] For Schleiermacher, true religion must be articulated in terms of each individual's own religious sentiments. Also, he insists again and again that the plurality of religious denominations is indeed necessary and indispensable, because the multiplicity of religions is grounded in the very essence of the personal religious experience.[4] As a matter of fact, he encourages his readers to develop their own religious positions within the context of a given religious denomination.

After his treatment of Christ, Schleiermacher spends a considerable amount of time setting out his doctrine of the Christian church. He declares that whenever believing persons are in proximity to one another, some kind of fellowship necessarily arises.[5] This fellowship grows as various clusters are gradually incorporated. The church is formed by the coming together of believing, regenerated individuals who then unite in mutual cooperation. Those who are elected and respond to the preaching of the gospel are touched by the Holy Spirit, who is the energizer of the Christian fellowship.[6] In the process of regeneration, each person becomes a new creature. Although there is a lack of equality regarding the distribution of graces flowing from the divine good pleasure, Schleiermacher is convinced that there is no such thing as a permanent exclusion of some from the divine favor, for that would be incompatible with God's mercy and justice.[7] Schleiermacher was of the opinion that those who do not participate in the salvation of Christ might possibly simply cease to exist after their deaths. Or perhaps even those worthy non-Christians might well attain a certain level of happiness after death through the faithful use of their natural lights.

Schleiermacher teaches that the Holy Spirit is the common spirit animating the community life of believers. The power at work within the church for uniting the regenerate as a community proceeds from the Holy Spirit, and this power is not to be found outside the Christian church.[8] Further, this Spirit operates in all believers. "Every regenerate person participates of the Holy Spirit, so that there is no living fellowship with Christ without an indwelling of the Holy Spirit, and vice versa."[9] This possession of the Spirit brings the life and actions of Christ into our memory and in some sense glorifies him in us. "The Christian Church, animated by the Holy Spirit, is in its purity and integrity the perfect image of the Redeemer, and each regenerate individual is an indispensable constituent of this fellowship."[10]

According to Schleiermacher, the fellowship of believers maintains a consistent attitude toward Christ and the Spirit. However, its relationship to the world does undergo modifications from time to time. He notes that the fellowship of Christians does vary its configuration in a given place depending on the culture and the history of that location. Also, the variations in the character and habits of people frequently call forth a distinct emphasis according to the situation. The changeable features in the church occur because it exists in a changing world.[11]

The presence of Christ in the church that lives in the Scriptures and in the ministry of the Word remains ever the same. Through baptism and the Lord's Supper, the fellowship of Christ is maintained and strengthened, while the governance of the church's life is managed through the power of the keys. Baptism initiates what Schleiermacher terms a conscious living fellowship with Christ, and the Lord's Supper constitutes a high moment in our union with the Redeemer. The power of the keys focuses on the forgiveness of sins and the correct ordering of the life of the church. Further, through the ministry of the Word, the prophetic or teaching function of the Lord expands throughout the world. The New Testament represents the first and the foundational expression of the Christian faith, which stands as the *norma normans* for all time. It is important to recall, however, that because the Holy Spirit is showered upon every successive generation, every age speaks its unique message into the fellowship and into the world. Nonetheless, Schleiermacher reminds his readers that the New Testament Scriptures remain the standard for every generation.[12]

Regarding the ministry of the Word, there are special qualities and gifts that are shared by the regular ministry, which Schleiermacher describes as a specific office entrusted to certain persons. This office involves definite responsibilities that are indispensable to the church. Schleiermacher warns, however, that the evolution of the clergy into a self-contained corporation that propagates itself has no biblical foundation whatsoever.[13] Although he affirms that set responsibilities are to be conferred on certain ministers for various functions in fixed locations, such matters are to be dealt with in what Schleiermacher refers to as practical theology rather than true dogmatics. The crucial matter is that the public gatherings for worship and preaching be established, while the appointment of members for leadership is really a secondary issue. Creeds and confessions of faith are necessary so that the fellowship of believers remains in conformity with the directives provided by the Holy Spirit. These confessions only have validity to the extent that their biblical character is evident. Schleiermacher stresses that the public ministers need not necessarily constitute a separate class within the church. Actually, the distinction between ordinary and clerical members should be kept to a minimum, because these separations are unhealthy for the fellowship.

The rite of baptism is the reception ceremony for entrance into the church. It is an act of Christ himself when performed in accordance with his direction and initiates the process of salvation for the recipient. Baptism applies the decree of redemption to the individual and formally admits the subject into fellowship with all the other believers.[14] Schleiermacher affirms that the degree of regeneration for each individual is difficult to determine, because it depends on his or her actual state of mind and heart. He emphasizes that the rite of baptism does not really effect an inward transformation, since it is only a sign of entrance into the fellowship of the faithful. According to one's disposition, however, baptism can have some effect on the remission of sin and also confers citizenship in the church along with the pledge of salvation.

As long as baptism is administered correctly by sprinkling or immersion, along with the proper biblical formula, it is valid and true regardless of the church that performs it. However, the faith of the person to be baptized is essential. Infant baptism is considered to be complete or fully effective only after the individual's profession of faith.[15] In fact, if the individual is already a believer, baptism really adds or contributes nothing. Schleiermacher insists that we must baptize children so that they can find their place in the fellowship, although the full effectiveness of infant baptism is achieved only after the person is capable of professing his or her faith. Confirmation, although not a sacrament, is intended to represent this rite of passage.

So that our fellowship might be strengthened and fortified, we are asked to participate in the Lord's Supper, which allows us to share in the body and blood of the Redeemer. This makes us more open to the saving influence of Christ—and because others are participating in the same experience, we also become more closely united with them. According to Schleiermacher, participation in the bread and wine does indeed involve a spiritual participating in the flesh and blood of Christ.[16] The Evangelical view, however, insists that the presence of the body and blood of Christ is realized only in the actual celebration of the sacrament. Therefore, the adoration of the consecrated elements outside of the context of the celebration of the sacrament is inappropriate.

Participation in the body and blood of Christ in the celebration of the sacrament confirms our fellowship with Christ and "the passing over of Christ's life into ours."[17] Schleiermacher seems to prefer Zwingli's view that participation in Christ's flesh and blood is only spiritual. This explanation, for Schleiermacher, seems to be the clearest and most workable—leaving the essence of the real presence to be debated by others.[18] In and through the Lord's Supper, we experience the forgiveness of sin and a deepening participation in the fellowship of believers. If we are guilty of unworthy participation in the Lord's Supper, we bring judgment upon ourselves. The word sacrament is only to be used for baptism and the Lord's Supper. The other rituals, such as absolution, orders, and extreme unction, are not sacramental.

Flowing from the power of the keys, a legislative and an administrative function in the church is grounded in the royal office of Christ.[19] Who is to be admitted and who is to be expelled relates to the use of the office of the keys. Although the church can require certain actions and prohibit other activities, the presumption must always be for liberty. Nonetheless, the existence of a body of laws of conduct remains an indispensable function of the church. This power resides in the ministry as a whole and ultimately in the entire fellowship of believers. It is critical that the distinction between the ministers and the laity not be unduly stressed, because that divides rather than unifies the fellowship. We learn from the early chapters of Acts that the whole congregation shared in the critical tasks of the body of believers (Acts 1:15–23; 6:2–6). Schleiermacher introduces the subject of prayer, and specifically prayer in the name of Jesus, which we are promised will be heard. It would be wrong, however, to pray that God's purpose will be altered and our own wishes accomplished instead. Rather, our prayer must be directed toward the pursuit of God's will and the growth of God's kingdom.

The invisible church includes the entire body of all the individuals who are regenerate and who constitute one great, undivided unity. On the other hand, the visible church consists of those who have accepted the gospel and who have responded to the gracious influences that they have received in a certain congregation. While the invisible church is essentially one, the visible church has been subjected to many separations and divisions. Nonetheless, there is in Schleiermacher's judgment a persistent drive toward unification that can be seen in the visible communities. These divisions are to be considered merely temporary, because the Holy Spirit is constantly working within the various bodies to bring them all together.[20] We are to revere and respect our own denominations but anticipate the day when all the Christian churches will come together in one abiding fellowship. In the meantime, we must do the very best we can to forge bonds of unity and collaboration with the other Christian churches and to emphasize any and all common elements between or among our congregations in the hope that we shall someday become one.

In each unit of the visible church resides an appreciation of Scripture and the ministry of the Word of God. Certain inspired individuals can indeed exert a reforming influence within their fellowship. Although individual churches may err in their formal presentation of doctrine, the errors will eventually be removed by the persistent witness of the truth that continues to live in the fellowship. There is, however, no definition of doctrine that is to be considered irreformable. According to Schleiermacher, the Evangelical churches are not to accept all the creeds promulgated by the ecumenical councils. There have been times when error seemed to prevail, but the truth eventually came forward to replace the error.[21]

Before the coming of Christ, the human race was living under what could be called preparatory grace that somehow reflected the divine righteousness. As Christianity has spread among the nations, it seems to be alone among religious bodies in terms of its worldwide extension. Schleiermacher hoped that this growth would continue to bring the message of salvation and the blessings of Christ to everyone.

Schleiermacher's masterwork, *The Christian Faith*, continues to exert considerable influence among Lutherans, Reformed believers, and countless Christians throughout the world. He has little to say about the organizational dimensions of the church. Perhaps this is because he wished his study to appeal to both the Lutheran and the Reformed traditions, and thus he left the specific details of ecclesiastical polity to what he called practical theology—for example, the details of church organization above the level of the parochial community.

Karl Barth (1886–1968)

Although Karl Barth's most extensive presentation of the doctrine of the church can be found in the second part of volume 4 of his *Church Dogmatics*, published in German in 1955, it is interesting to look at his views on the subject as briefly outlined in the first of his three credos, which appeared in 1935. This was just three years after the first half-volume of his *Church Dogmatics* was completed.[22] Chapter 14 of the 1935 *Credo* deals with his thoughts on the subject before his full presentation of ecclesiology. He refers to the church as an assembly that comes together as the result of a call. These people share a common interest. It is a holy community because of its singular dignity and the special commission placed upon it. Barth refers to it as a catholic community because its principal interests are everywhere the same. The primitive church came into being through the bestowal of the Holy Spirit on the apostles on Pentecost. There are some who insist that the church must be organized democratically, while others hold that it must be a monarchy. Barth declares that the church of Jesus Christ is to be governed by the Word of God himself.[23] It is nothing less than the kingdom of God between Christ's first and second coming.

The commission of the church is primarily focused on the tasks of preaching the gospel and the administration of the sacraments, which Barth identifies as the ministry of the Word of God. All other functions of the church must be secondary compared with this mission. The true church, that is, those who are living members of the body of Christ, are known only to God, whereas the visible church is the society of those who are its members by outward confession.[24] Barth recognizes the Reformed church and the Lutheran Church as the true church of Jesus. However, the Roman Catholic Church and the neo-Protestant churches are not to be included within the true church.

In the second half of volume 1, *The Doctrine of the Word of God*, published in German in 1955, Barth lays the groundwork for his later treatment of the church. He affirms that the Word of God is present and active always. It is actualized again and again.

> The present-day witnesses of the Word of God can and should look back to the witnesses of the same Word that preceded them

and away to those contemporary with them. In this matter it is impossible to speak without having first heard. All speaking is a response to these fathers and brethren. Therefore these fathers and brethren have a definite authority, the authority of prior witnesses of the Word of God, who have to be respected as such. . . . Second, this confession includes a confession that the witness of the presence of the church has a definite authority to the extent that it is the witness of the living and present Word of God. . . .[25]

When the church speaks, it gives a human form to the Word of God, and this confession of the Word presumes a confession of the church's authority. It is not an authority that constitutes a form of self-government. The Evangelical church is the church of obedience, and not one that is self-governed. Christ has called the church into life and maintains it in life. For Barth, the teaching office of the church is unable to speak infallible truth through its papal mouthpiece or in neo-Protestantism through its modern consciousness of self and history, which filters the Word. The word that the church must speak is none other than the Word of biblical witness. It is the Word that stands over against the authority of the church.[26] There must always be a subordination to the prophetic and apostolic Word revealed in Scripture, which alone has divine authority in the church. According to Barth, the decision for the primacy of Scripture is the decision for the reformation of the church.

With Scripture, the Christian church possesses and exercises genuine authority. To the extent that it is obedient and responsive to the Word of God, the church can speak with authority. The church is continually brought into being by hearing and receiving God's Word.[27] Confessing our faith is the act in which we receive from one another and respond in faith to hearing the Word of God. Before we speak, we must listen to the confession of others who lived before us and to the confession of our contemporaries. When we articulate the faith, we must submit our confession to the judgment of the believing church. According to Barth: "The authority of the Church is the confession of the Church in the narrowest meaning of the concept, i.e., the voice of others in the Church reaching me in specific agreements and common declarations and as such preceding my own faith and the confessing of it. Church authority always consists in the documented presence of such agreements."[28]

Barth discusses in some detail the development of the biblical canon. The early church had numerous discussions on the subject and early on decided which books were to be included in the authentic canon. We had to be informed by the primitive church which writings were to be considered as God's Word. Over the years, there have been formulations of various theological positions, and some are more important than others. The Reformers did not accept the entire theological hierarchy of the church fathers as a second source of revelation, although certain ones such as Augustine have been considered witnesses of the truth by the Evangelical church, although always subject to the norm of the Scriptures.

Luther and Calvin became for the Reformers the critical heralds of gospel teaching in the sixteenth century, ranking with any of the early fathers, even Augustine. Their authority is similar to the authority of the church fathers in Roman Catholicism. Barth declares that Calvin's authority was less dependent on his personality than Luther's. It is almost entirely grounded in his teachings. The words of Luther and Calvin are essential for the existence and life of the Evangelical church.[29] It is interesting that Barth did not consider Friedrich Schleiermacher a church father or an essential church witness in the nineteenth century: "In spite of the greatness of his achievement and the intensity of his influence, the theology of Schleiermacher becomes only the starting-point and center of an esoteric tradition in the Evangelical Church. . . . Schleiermacher did not find any successor among the leading theologians of the 19th century."[30] Barth observes that Schleiermacher raised neo-Protestantism, with its concern for self and historical development, to its full maturity.

The Reformed confessions of the sixteenth century can be compared with the creeds of the early church councils in terms of importance. Barth was especially impressed by the Augsburg Confession of 1530. A confession is a formulation forged out of a common discussion and decision and proposed as a statement of faith to be professed by believers. Its authority depends on how fully it reflects the message of the Scriptures. These confessions were ordinarily formulated in a moment of conflict, such as the declaration of Nicaea I (325) against Arius. Not all church confessions are universally acknowledged. Although the Roman Catholics revere solemn pronouncements of dogma as bearing the weight of Scripture, Barth teaches that, for Evangelicals, confessions are considered to be important and binding until such time as they are succeeded by subsequent declarations.[31] Even the most honored of church confessions should never be allowed to be elevated to the dignity and binding character of divine revelation. The authority of confessions is to be considered a stage on the road to an ever-fuller understanding of divine truth.

Barth's early presentation of the authority of the Word and authority under the Word serves as a foundation for his full treatment of the church in volume 4, part 2 of *Church Dogmatics*. This volume, *The Doctrine of Reconciliation*, was originally published in German in 1955, with the English translation appearing in 1958.[32] In the preface to the work, Barth speaks of the "long journey" of the *Church Dogmatics*, and comments that only the angels know if and when it will be entirely completed. He was approaching his seventieth birthday and began to wonder himself if his massive work would ever be concluded.

Barth writes that the Holy Spirit brings about the edification of the Christian church. More precisely, Jesus, through the efforts of the quickening power of the Holy Spirit, builds up the church in the world. The time of the church is situated between the resurrection and the return of Christ. The Augsburg Confession describes the church as the congregation of the saints in which the gospel is purely taught and the sacraments rightly administered.[33] Although we can see the members of the church and its officials, we can never see the true church, because it is not immediately visible but can be seen only in faith. The goal of the church as described by Barth "is to give a provisional representation of the sanctification of all humanity and human life as it has taken place in Christ."[34] The community is ordained to express this provisional representation. Barth insists that there are no superior and inferior roles or functions in the Christian community. God himself is the true builder who works through Jesus and in the power of the Spirit. The directions and counsels of the apostles must serve to guide the church, and each single member is to share in the task of the edification of the community. What keeps the church together is the mutual love among its members. The acts of common worship generate the vitality prompting and fostering the growth of the body. From the warm center of common worship, the spirit and the activity spread out into every phase of the lives of believers.

The church of Christ has but one objective, and that is the proclamation of the good news of the kingdom. It is necessary for the membership of the church to grow, although the quality of its members is more critical than growth in numbers. Barth concedes, however, that the actual growth of the Christian fellowship has been surprising indeed.[35] The risen Lord continues to be active in the fellowship through the quickening power of the Holy Spirit. Christ's earthly form, his body, is the community of believers, although he is not confined within the community or limited by it.

Barth warns that there is a danger to the body of believers from the world around it, which at times attempts to eliminate it and at other times to make it ineffective and inept. The danger from within can be the growth of secularization when it holds to a particular philosophy in its presentation of the Word of God. This controls and stifles the power of the Word so that it is incapable of realizing its true potential. The Word is thus inhibited in its role as the transforming agent of the Christian fellowship and the world. The second danger is self-glorification when the church substitutes its own limited and provincial objectives in place of the direction of the Holy

Spirit. This can occur when ecclesiastical authorities pursue their own private goals and become enamored of their own status and importance. When these perils arise, we can be confident that a faithful remnant will always persevere and eventually lead the fellowship back to the true course.

Karl Barth then directs his attention to the form in which the growth and maturation of the community will be realized. Such form or shape cannot be indefinite or haphazard and must possess its own order. The order and form are achieved through the establishment of certain definite relationships among the members within the fellowship. This involves the orderly distribution of obligations and functions among the members and the establishment of leadership roles so that the responsibilities and rights of all the members can be equitably and efficiently distributed and coordinated.

> It is also a matter of the relationship of individual Christian congregations to other congregations both near and distant; of the preservation and exercise of reciprocity in action and therefore of mutual understanding; of a comprehensive direction which will coordinate their existence and action. . . . We cannot undertake to develop and answer in detail these questions of order. This is a matter for canon law rather than dogmatics. But dogmatics cannot refrain from considering the standpoints normative for canon law.[36]

The proper coordination of relationships between the ministers and the faithful and between the faithful with one another has to be determined by law and ordinance. Without law, there can be no order, and church life will quickly descend into confusion. In this context, the power of the Holy Spirit is frustrated. The issues of church law and church order are by no means matters of little importance, for confusion and lack of focus will surely result without a properly structured church order: "It is concretely to Scripture that the community has to listen in the question of law and order, in the conflict against ecclesiastical lawlessness and disorder. It has to receive direction from the Bible."[37] Barth advises that Scripture constitutes the *norma normans* concerning the intent and direction of authentic church organization. The Christian fellowship is truly a sociological construct that is one human society among others. As such, it comes into contact with the civil government, which exercises some jurisdiction over it. However, the church must not allow the civil authorities to control its doctrine, its preaching, or its theology.[38]

Barth makes clear that his only purpose is to lay out certain general principles that point to the direction that ecclesiastical legislation and church order should take.

> We cannot develop the law itself. This is a matter of different Churches in different places and times and situations, and it may often demand special legal knowledge and skill in addition to the necessary theological insights. There is, of course, this basic law, and its analysis will yield certain general presuppositions which underlie all Church law. But there is no such thing as universal Church law.[39]

The basic law to which Barth refers is the Christian law of service, "For the Son of Man came not to be served but to serve, and to give his life as a ransom for many" (Mark 10:45). The community achieves its destined order when it dedicates itself wholeheartedly to the service of others.

This law of service is universal and always applicable in the Christian church. Each and every believer must be engaged in some form of service to others. The role of canon law according to Barth is to distribute the different functions and responsibilities to various members of the community. He is convinced that it is in the area of liturgical organization that law has its original seat.[40] The living center of the community must be its worship and, through worship, its true identity is manifested in the world.

> In divine service it becomes and is itself a witness to its own being, to its determination in the world, to the factuality of its existence. And in divine service it exists and acts prophetically in relation to the world to the extent that in divine service—and here alone directly—there is a serious discharge of its commission to be a provisional representation of humanity as it is sanctified in Jesus Christ.[41]

For Barth, all law is to be grounded in the event of divine worship, "For where two or three are gathered in my name, I am there among them" (Matt 18:20). He lays out four basic observations governing the relationship between law and worship:

1. While two or three gather together to listen to the Word of God, their response should be a public response, and this is actually a confession of faith.

2. This listening and responding together creates a genuine fraternity, because they all share a common faith grounded in their common baptism.

3. They eat and drink together as brothers and sisters with the risen Lord presiding at the table. He gives himself to them as an example of the communion of saints.

4. He invites them to pray together, for communal prayer is indispensable. Their common prayer inspires those in attendance to action and to mission; this is the origin of church discipline.[42]

Church ordinances must be influenced by the spirit of the times.

> It is actually the case that this law, as and because it is living law, demands constant re-investigation by a community which is open for new direction and instruction (not from below but from above), and is therefore willing and ready for new answers. . . . Even more concretely, they must be answers which involve the establishment and execution of ecclesiastical and congregational ordinances in which one thing is commanded, another forbidden, and a third permitted, or left to free and responsible judgment within certain limits in which explicit decisions are made according to the best of our knowledge and conscience.[43]

Barth reminds his readers that although these ordinances and enactments are necessary and must be codified, they are nothing more than human law. They are therefore subject to perpetual reform and revision and must be put aside when a better arrangement surfaces.

> No Church order is perfect, for none has fallen directly from heaven and none is identical with the basic law of the Christian community. Even the orders of the primitive New Testament community (whatever form they took) were not perfect, nor are those of the Western Papacy, the Eastern Patriarchate, the Synodal Presbyterianism which derives from Calvin's system, Anglican, Methodist, Neo-Lutheran and other forms of Episcopacy, or Congregationalism with its sovereignty of the individual community. Nor are the orders of all different systems which are derivative variations of these basic types. There is no reason to look down proudly and distastefully from one to the others. At one time they may all have been living law sought and in a certain exaggeration found in obedience, and therefore legitimate forms of the body of Jesus Christ. Indeed they may be this still. Thus for all the problems to which they give rise they must be respected by the others.[44]

Individual churches are urged to be open and ready to learn by comparing with their own the different forms and structures of church order found among the various congregations. The organizational shape of the church enables the various members to relate to one another, to perform their respective tasks, and to grow together in the image of Christ. By means of its organizational fabric, the church represents itself as a corporate apostle to the world, for it owes Christian witness to those outside. But each church must ever keep in mind that what it owes to the world is not a legal system but the gospel. The organizational pattern of the church is merely intended to reflect the power of the good news to those within and around it.

Churches must be mindful that the order of the legal structure of the ecclesial body can on occasion learn from secular organizations. In this connection, Barth instructs his readers:

> In its encounter with the world it may sometimes happen that in this particular field the children of the world prove to be wiser than the children of light, so that in the question concerning its law the Church has reason to learn from the world (which does not know what it knows), receiving from the witness which it ought to give. For all its awareness of the independence of its task, it cannot exclude this possibility.[45]

Colm O'Grady describes Barth's views on the organizational varieties to be found in the Christian churches.

> God's Word is free to use existing social forms and make them, without changing them in themselves, a specific society, the visible form of His community. As He does this He permits and commands His community to choose its own form. There is none it must select, and none it must refuse. . . . It may be a monarchical, aristocratic or democratic Church; it may be a national, state, or free Church; it must always be a confessing and missionary Church, witnessing in its visibility to its invisible essence.[46]

Paul Tillich (1886–1965)

Before coming to the United States in 1933, Paul Tillich taught philosophy and theology at the universities of Marburg, Dresden, Leipzig, and Frankfort. His difficulties with the National Socialist Party in Germany became so severe that he was asked to leave Germany. In America, Tillich taught at Union Theological Seminary in New York City, Harvard, and the University of Chicago. His masterpiece, *Systematic Theology*, was published over a period of twelve years, with the third and final volume appearing in 1963. Great numbers of his pupils find that his many published sermons are an excellent introduction to his theology. His collections of sermons, *The Shaking of the Foundations* (1948) and *The New Being* (1955), are still widely read and deeply appreciated. Tillich's monograph *Dynamics of Faith* (1957) was considered by the Lutheran theologian Wilhelm Pauck (d. 1981) to be the finest popular introduction to his theology.

One of Tillich's most influential concepts is the idea of the New Being revealed in Christ. It heralds a New Creation that has occurred with Christ, and all of us are summoned to participate in it.

> We want only to show you something we have seen and to tell you something we have heard: That in the midst of the old creation there is a New Creation, and this New Creation is manifest in Jesus who is called the Christ. . . . We should worry more about it than about anything else between heaven and earth. The New Creation—this is our ultimate concern; this should be our infinite passion—the infinite passion of every human being. . . . And if the Church which is the assembly of God has an ultimate significance, this is its significance: That here the reunion of man to man is pronounced and confessed and realized, even if in fragments, weaknesses and distortions.[47]

The New Being is defined in three words:

1. *Reconciliation*, that is, the elimination of all hostility within ourselves, against others, and against God.

2. The *New Creation* is the reality in which the separated are reunited. In Christ, there is never any separation or division between God, his fellow men, or within himself.

3. *Resurrection*—the power of the New Being to create life in us out of death, not just at some future time, but in the present.

Tillich describes God as the Ground of Being, and he insists that the divine Spirit is ever present to the human spirit. Mankind has never been abandoned by God, for we are always under the influence of the Spiritual Presence who breaks into the human spirit and drives the human spirit beyond itself.[48] We are always able to participate in "the transcendent union of unambiguous life."[49] Although this participation is partial and incomplete, the acceptance of the Divine Spirit (God) on the part of a believing group constitutes a community as a holy convocation. The Divine Spirit was present and active in Jesus during his earthly life. God was in him so completely that we call him the Christ, "the historical embodiment of the New Being for all mankind."[50]

Jesus was apprehended by the Spirit at the moment of his baptism, becoming the bearer of the Spirit without any limit. Tillich insists that the Spiritual Presence in Jesus is what propels and drives his individual spirit. After the risen Christ returned to the Father, the Spirit takes his place on earth in order to reveal all the wondrous implications and dimensions of his appearance (John 16:12–14). Tillich is fond of the term "Spiritual Community" and frequently substitutes it for the word church, inasmuch as the latter term has been weighted down with a good number of negative connotations throughout the centuries.[51] The Spiritual Community is nothing less than a creature of the Divine Spirit. It is authentic and unambiguous to the extent that it is grounded in the New Being that has appeared in Christ.

According to Tillich, the Spiritual Community possesses five marks, which he enumerates as follows:

1. the ecstatic quality it manifested at the moment of its creation (Acts 1 and 2);

2. the spontaneous proclamation of faith in the risen Christ as the New Being (Acts 2:22–35);

3. the overpowering appearance of a love that grows into mutual service (Acts 4:27–34);

4. the sudden explosion of unity among various nations and languages present at the Pentecost event;

5. the birth of universality revealed in the missionary fervor coming almost immediately out of the Pentecost experience.[52]

In addition to the Christian churches, for Tillich there are other communities that reveal the power of the New Being, such as various youth groups and a number of cultural and political movements. Moreover, many individuals who are not members of such groups manifest to the world around them the power of the Spiritual Presence. When this power takes hold of persons and groups, it begets what Tillich calls unambiguous life, although in a fragmentary manner. The various Christian churches reveal the Spiritual Community in a formally religious manner, while the other groups reveal the Spiritual Community in a latent state, because the faith and love of Christ are not explicitly reflected out of them.

For Tillich, the people of Israel constitute a latent spiritual unity, as do the devotional communities of Islam. Because of this, they embody the Spiritual Presence and form a part of the Spiritual Community. There is a difference between the Spiritual Community and the kingdom of God, which is to achieve its ultimate fulfillment at the end of time. The churches represent the Spiritual Community as being partly actual and partly in potency, for their life is still ambiguous as Tillich views them. The Spiritual Community is a power and an invisible structure that lives within the various religious congregations. Such groups are called churches if they are formally grounded in the New Being that is revealed in Christ. If they have other foundations, they are called by other names, such as synagogues, cult groups, or movements of various kinds.[53]

In Tillich's teaching, the Spiritual Community is really the very essence of the churches, and the origin of everything that constitutes them as ecclesiastical bodies. The churches are holy because of the existence of the New Being that is present in them. While the Roman Church proclaims institutional holiness, the Protestants are not as willing to predicate holiness of their churches.[54] However, the Spiritual Presence remains operative in all the congregations through the medium of prophetic criticism and the spirit of reformation that lives on in them.

The second quality of the churches is unity, which the World Council of Churches has seriously attempted to promote even before its first General Assembly in 1948. Tillich attests that even if it were able to create an entity such as the United Churches of the World, there is little doubt that new divisions would soon appear. The third quality of the Christian churches is universality, although this goal has never actually been achieved. The Orthodox are limited in their outreach through their strong ties to the Byzantine culture. Rome is limited by its canon law and the institution of the papacy. Also, the subjection of other religions and cultures to Western civilization has been the weakness of Protestantism.[55]

In the judgment of Tillich, the widespread imposition of creeds has placed a burden of sorts on faithful believers, which forces them to limit their belief structure within certain confines. Because of this, members are often not especially interested in retaining their membership, although in most cases they cannot imagine not belonging. They are inclined to have misgivings concerning their continuing allegiance. The Protestant churches must be aware that they cannot hold exclusively to a particular doctrinal tradition, because they can thereby violate the venerable Protestant principle of freedom and the right of free expression. Protestantism is also rather slow to insist on definite canons of discipline because of the many hierarchical abuses in the Christian past. Further, there are serious misgivings among the Protestants concerning any excommunication of members, because no human religious organization should impose itself between God and the adherents of the community. Moreover, there is usually a deep anxiety in churches with a definite creed and order of life that the potential follower who wishes to be taken into the community may weaken the body by introducing elements of profanation.

For Tillich, there are three distinct ecclesiastical functions. The first has to do with the church's radical stand as a vehicle of reformation. The sixteenth-century Reformation occurred because the Roman Church repressed this activity at a time when the prophetic Spirit called for a reformation of the church "in head and members." The reforming spirit is the corrective against absolutism that represses the dynamic essence of the church, which strives always for the freedom of the sons and daughters of God. The danger of absolutism and the refusal to adapt must be resisted in all its forms. "The church shows its presence as church only if the Spirit breaks into the finite forms and drives them beyond themselves."[56]

In addition, the church must always be in a receptive mood regarding its institutional forms and structures. It must not become a static hierarchical entity that claims it has received its institutional shape once and for all and will never change or allow for new directions. For Tillich, no organizational arrangement, not even the offices and the patterns of ministry, follow necessarily from the nature of the church. The church that remains rigid in its organizational forms can easily distance itself from the flow of history. This receptive function eliminates the possibility of the development of a fixed hierarchical group that mediates while all others merely receive.[57]

Another important function of the church is the ever-expanding role of mission, because it is responsive to the universalist dimension of the church's message. Evangelism is to be directed toward those outside the church communion and to those who have ceased to become active members. Practical apologetics must be viewed as a constant emphasis in the life of the spiritual community. The church's cognitive function involves the theological enterprise, which can be developed based on any philosophical tradition. The essentialist direction, following such scholars as Kant and Hegel, centers on the structure and the fabric of reality, while the existentialist approach, following thinkers like Nietzsche and Heidegger, focuses on the range of problems arising out of the predicament of existing.

Tillich addresses what he terms the communal function of the church and its organizational patterns. He warns, "every system of religious hierarchies is conducive to social injustice." And he adds: "Even if there are no formal hierarchies there are degrees of importance in the church and the higher degrees are socially and economically dependent on and interrelated to the higher degrees in the social group. This is one of the reasons why in most cases the churches have supported the 'powers to be,' including their injustices against the lower classes."[58] Tillich emphasizes the importance of promoting the equality of all in the life of the church, and he notes that this equality is given special emphasis in the Letter of James 2:1–8.

Religious leadership must be attentive to the question of equal treatment, for it is grounded in the equality of all before God. The organizational patterns in the churches must always be alert to this, for the equal treatment of all is indispensable. "The Spirit does not give constitutional rules, but it guides the churches toward a Spiritual use of sociologically adequate offices and institutions."[59] In Tillich's judgment, no church office, even those reflected in the New Testament, is the product of a mandate from the Divine Spirit. He affirms the Protestant principle of the fallibility of all religious institutions. In these organizational questions, it is simply a matter of "sociological adequacy, practical expediency and human wisdom."[60]

The priesthood of all believers must always hold a place of preeminence as a protest against any special order of priests or ministers. However, Tillich stands in opposition to what he calls subjective religiosity. He feels that there is no such thing as private religion, for the hermit and the recluse live on what they have assimilated from some religious group or congregation. The churches are sociological entities and must have continuous interaction with other social bodies, influencing and being influenced by them. However, the churches may never become servants of the state or lose their radical otherness, for then they become nothing more than social clubs.[61]

Paul Tillich's approach to ecclesiology is fraught with numerous ambiguities as to how the churches should present themselves in and to the world. The theologian Langdon Gilkey (1919–2004) has described Tillich's view of the ecclesial role as follows:

> The present church, therefore, is diffused with ambiguity as well as with grace, and it must await its own redemption before it can fulfill fully its own historical task. Nevertheless, its role is *in* the world, united with culture both in estrangement, in grace, and in promise. The New Being, to which it witnesses, is a gift to the *world*, to the world's *entire* life, and so to culture; the problems or contradictions that the New Being heals are the *world's* problems and contradictions; its promises are promises for the world. The present task of the church is, therefore, within culture, not apart from it. It is as much the task of nurturing, criticizing, and reshaping the religious substance of *culture* closer to the New Being it seeks to bear and to the Kingdom it proclaims as it is the task of nurturing and fostering the community of the *ecclesia*.[62]

Dietrich Bonhoeffer (1906–45)

Dietrich Bonhoeffer did his principal theological studies at Tübingen and at the University of Berlin, submitting his doctoral dissertation, *Sanctorum Communio*, in 1927.[63] He completed a second dissertation, *Act*

and Being, at New York's Union Theological Seminary in 1931. For the
next six years, Bonhoeffer occasionally taught at the University of Berlin
and at Union Theological. He also assumed several pastorates in London
and in Berlin. He became active in the Confessing Church that grew out
of the Barmen Declaration in 1934. The members of the Confessing
Church were opposed to the direction of the Nazi regime.

Sanctorum Communio approaches ecclesiology within the context of a
sociology of the church. It was published in German in 1930 and in
English in 1963. According to Bonhoeffer, there are two ways of misunderstanding the church. We can confuse it with a given religious congregation, or we can confuse it with the Realm (or the Kingdom) of God.[64]
He asks whether the Christian reality is fundamentally an ecclesiastical
community, or if it is possible to accept Christianity on a completely individual basis. His response is unambiguous. Only one religion holds the
idea of community as an integral and indispensable element, and that is
Christianity. For the Apostle Paul, the church community is verified in its
totality in each individual congregation. Because the church is Christ's
body, he is really present in the church, whose growth and expansion are
achieved by the spirit of Christ and the Holy Spirit.

To be "in Christ" is essentially to be in the church. The Holy Spirit is
the gathering force, bringing the ecclesial body together. As a corporate
social body, the church is visible, but as an eschatological entity, it is invisible. Christ is truly the Lord of this new humanity, which possesses a corporate personality.[65] Humanity under the headship of Adam is being
transformed into a new humanity in Christ. While the new humanity is
born in the Easter experience, the birth of the church is achieved at
Pentecost with the advent of the Holy Spirit. Jesus established a religious
community through the work of his apostles. For Bonhoeffer, the term
"kingdom of God" does not apply to the church because it is a specifically
eschatological concept. However, Christian love strives to realize God's
love everywhere. Bonhoeffer insists that community with God exists only
in the church, which is animated by the Holy Spirit.[66] Faith in Christ
involves faith in the church community, wherein a whole new set of social
relations has been created. Christ's love for us creates a new bond between
my neighbors and me.

In Bonhoeffer's judgment, Christians cannot live without the church.
One of the miracles of the church is that one person can forgive the sins
of another with priestly authority.[67] The gifts of the Holy Spirit unite the
members of the church community into a single collective person.
Bonhoeffer follows Luther in insisting that corporate congregational
prayer is a major source contributing to the unification of the congregations. The priesthood of all believers creates the critical unity bringing

together all the members into one body. All are to be considered equals, since all are animated by the grace of Christ. The church possesses a will of its own that guides the members and gives shape and form to the church's corporate presence.

For Bonhoeffer, the objective spirit of the collective body remains intact in spite of the fallibility and sinfulness of the church. It is the Holy Spirit who guarantees the effectiveness of the church's preaching and its sacramental activity. The body of the church includes the wheat and the chaff, which will be separated at the end of time. The empirical church, in Bonhoeffer's view, is composed of the many individual congregations that identify themselves as Christian communities. These various congregations form together a true unity in which there is one Spirit and one Word; these congregations together constitute a single body. The empirical church does not include anything more than the various individual congregations. There is no ecclesiastical superstructure that is part and parcel of the fabric of the church, because this would be contrary to Protestant thought.[68] Each single congregation is truly the body of Christ, and yet all coalesce into one collective entity.

The ministry of the word and the celebration of the sacraments are the principal functions of the church community, and God has promised to be ever present to each corporate body. Smaller house churches should not be encouraged at the expense of the local parishes because they dilute and weaken the presence of the church in those regions where they are too frequent. Bonhoeffer asks who has the responsibility for preaching the Word that needs to be spoken, not in terms of yesterday, but in terms of today's challenges. Although the Roman Catholic notions of priest and office are not applicable to the Protestant understanding of church, Bonhoeffer places his trust in the promise of Isaiah 55:10–11:

For as the rain and the snow come down from heaven,
and do not return until they have watered the earth,
making it bring forth and sprout, giving seed to the sower
and bread to the eater, so shall my word that goes out
from my mouth; it shall not return to me empty,
but it shall accomplish that which I purpose
and succeed in the thing for which I sent it.[69]

Placing the work of preaching the Word in the very center of worship is sufficient to achieve the efficacious result. The preacher articulates the objective spirit of the believing community in the appropriate forms that have become fixed according to what Bonhoeffer terms the prevailing theological consensus.

> In the Protestant church there is no theurgy, and no magical authority invested in the office or its bearers. The concept of the *priesthood of all believers* is merely another way of expressing this. The reality of the church-community which has only one head, namely Christ, protects us from the idea of a spiritual-earthly head. . . . Having thus defined the Protestant meaning of the concept of office as it relates to the objective spirit, and having found it appropriate, we have gained a deeper understanding of the organized individual congregation, which is held together by orderly assemblies around the word and the administration of the sacraments.[70]

For Bonhoeffer, the sacraments are nothing less than the purposeful acts of the church community itself. Since baptism is normally celebrated in the context of infant baptism, the subject receiving the sacrament is really the objective spirit of the church community. In the Lord's Supper, Christ's presence is not merely symbolic. The presence of Christ energizes believers, and all are given the right and the mission to act as priest for their fellow believers.[71] Preaching becomes the introduction to the celebration of the Lord's Supper. Bonhoeffer notes that baptism, preaching, and the Lord's Supper are each directed to an ever-smaller circle of adherents.

The Word is the absolute authority in the church and calls for absolute obedience. It is the sacred responsibility of the church to watch over the purity of the Word that it proclaims, whether it is set forth in the creed, in its theology, or in its scriptural exegesis. When the church speaks authoritatively, we are obliged to obey, except in the rare case when refusal to respond to the church's authority constitutes a supreme act of obedience.[72] For Bonhoeffer, the church cannot be considered a compulsory organization. Unlike the Roman Catholic understanding, the church cannot be viewed as having been directly established by God. Rather, an organized Protestant church is the result of an act of the believing community itself. Bonhoeffer prefers to see the church as a community of persons and not as a society.[73] The proper acts of this community are preaching and the administration of the sacraments.

The love that binds the community together is infused by the Holy Spirit, who is the very heart of the collective body. According to Bonhoeffer, the fabric of the family is somewhat comparable to the structure of the church, because love is the life principle of both. Although order and governance are to prevail in the church, the ultimate authority is grounded in the rule of the Word. While the Roman Catholic concept of church assumes a link between Spirit and office, Protestants place a necessary connection between the Spirit and the church community. For Bonhoeffer, this amounts to a fundamental sociological difference.

> But then what does it mean "to believe in the church"? We do not believe in an invisible church nor in the Realm of God within the church as a *coetus electorum* (company of the elect). Instead we believe that God has made the concrete, empirical church (*Kirche*) in which the word is preached and the sacraments are celebrated to be God's own church-community (*Gemeinde*). . . . We believe in the church as the church of God, as the community of saints, those who are sanctified by God. We believe, however, that this takes place always within the historical framework of the empirical church.[74]

The church is one because of the one Lord who is operative in it. It is holy because of the Holy Spirit who is its animating force. It is catholic because it is intended to embrace the whole of humankind. Although Bonhoeffer did not attempt to take a definite stand on the issue of *apocatastasis* (i.e., the final and complete salvation of all), he did treat the idea somewhat favorably: "The strongest reason for accepting the idea of apocatastasis would seem to me that all Christians must be aware of having brought sin into the world, and thus aware of being bound together with the whole of humanity in sin, aware of having the sins of humanity on their conscience."[75] However, Bonhoeffer warns: "This precludes from the outset any mystical ideas such as a final assimilation into God's all-encompassing person, a fusion of our supposedly divine nature with that of God."[76] In the end time, the work of the church will have been completed. Then Christ will hand over his church to the Father that God may be all in all (1 Cor 15:24).

Dietrich Bonhoeffer published his most popular work, *Discipleship*, in 1937.[77] It was originally issued in German, and an abridged English version entitled *The Cost of Discipleship* appeared in 1949. In it, his theology of church is essentially the same as the presentation in *Sanctorum Communio*. According to Bonhoeffer, in the risen body of Christ, all of humanity has been truly accepted by God. Since Christ bore our sin, he was able to forgive our sinfulness.[78] Jesus became the fountainhead of the new humanity. We in turn acquire a share in the community of the body of Christ through baptism and the Lord's Supper. The body of Christ is now identified with the new humanity. "Outside the church there is only the old internally divided human being."[79] The role of the Holy Spirit is to offer Christ to believers who then complete the sufferings of Jesus in and through their daily lives. The church community becomes visible through the preaching of the Word, which is apostolic to the extent that it is grounded in the very witness of the prophets and the apostles. The Holy Spirit ignites faith in the hearers. The visibility of the church is given its final configuration through baptism and the Lord's Supper.

Bonhoeffer points out that various congregations call for different offices and ministries to answer the needs and the purposes of the respective churches. The New Testament refers to apostles, prophets, teachers, bishops, deacons, and other officials. This variety is reflected in the operation of the many Christian communities, which remain at liberty to change functions and functionaries according to their needs. Regarding the office of preaching, communities must always be on their guard against deviant and heretical ministers, who are to be deprived of their ministries and cast out of their churches so that the Christian message can be preserved in its authentic form.

In one or two of his *Letters and Papers from Prison*, written in 1944, Bonhoeffer speaks of a religionless Christianity. "What do a church, a community, a sermon, a liturgy, or Christian life mean in a religionless world? . . . In that case, Christ is no longer an object of religion, but something quite different, really the Lord of the world. But what does that mean? What is the place of worship and prayer in a religionless situation?"[80] For one who had dedicated his life to the study of the church, these observations are difficult to reconcile with the recurring themes of his ecclesiology as laid out in *Sanctorum Communio* (1930). The enormous religious and political turmoil in Germany during the 1930s and early 1940s no doubt affected his thinking, which remains an excellent reflection of that most trying time. Because of his involvement in a failed attack against the life of Adolf Hitler, Bonhoeffer was hanged in the concentration camp at Flossenbürg, Germany, on April 9, 1945, just weeks before the German surrender ending World War II in Europe.

Notes

1. B. A. Gerrish, *Tradition and the Modern World: Reformed Theology in the Nineteenth Century* (Chicago: University of Chicago Press, 1978), 20–21.

2. Friedrich Schleiermacher, *On Religion: Speeches to Its Cultured Despisers* (trans. Richard Crouter; Cambridge, UK: Cambridge University Press, 1988; repr., 2000), 76.

3. Ibid., 90.

4. Ibid., 96.

5. Schleiermacher, *The Christian Faith* (trans. from 2d German ed.; ed. H. R. MacKintosh and J. S. Stewart; Edinburgh: T&T Clark, 1986), 525.

6. Ibid., 535.

7. Ibid., 544.

8. Ibid., 570.

9. Ibid., 574.

10. Ibid., 578.

11. Ibid., 585.

12. Ibid., 604.

13. Ibid., 615.

14. Ibid., 622.

15. Ibid., 633.

16. Ibid., 644.

17. Ibid., 652.

18. Ibid., 649.

19. Ibid., 660.

20. Ibid., 686.

21. Ibid., 692.

22. Karl Barth, *Credo* (New York: Scribner's, 1962).

23. Ibid., 146.

24. Ibid., 147.

25. Karl Barth, *The Doctrine of the Word of God* (vol. 1, pt. 2 of *Church Dogmatics*; trans. G. T. Thomson and H. Knight; New York: Scribner's, 1956), 573.

26. Ibid., 579.

27. Ibid., 588.

28. Ibid., 593.

29. Ibid., 609.

30. Ibid., 610.

31. Ibid., 657.

32. Karl Barth, *The Doctrine of Reconciliation* (vol. 4, pt. 2 of *Church Dogmatics*; trans. G. W. Bromiley; ed. G. W. Bromiley and T. F. Torrance; Edinburgh: T&T Clark, 1958).

33. Ibid., 618.

34. Ibid., 620.

35. Ibid., 650.

36. Ibid., 678.

37. Ibid., 683.

38. Ibid., 689.

39. Ibid., 690.

40. Ibid., 695.

41. Ibid., 698.

42. Ibid., 699–710.

43. Ibid., 711.

44. Ibid., 718.

45. Ibid., 725.

46. Colm O'Grady, *The Church in the Theology of Karl Barth* (Washington, DC: Corpus Books, 1968), 313.

47. Paul Tillich, *The New Being* (New York: Scribner's, 1955), 18, 19, 23.

48. Tillich, *Systematic Theology* (vol. 3; Chicago: University of Chicago Press, 1967), 112.

49. Ibid., 140.

50. Ibid., 144.

51. Ibid., 149.

52. Ibid., 151.

53. Ibid., 162.

54. Ibid., 168.

55. Ibid., 170.

56. Ibid., 187.

57. Ibid., 189.

58. Ibid., 205.

59. Ibid., 207.

60. Ibid.

61. Ibid., 216.

62. Langdon Gilkey, "The Role of the Theologian in Contemporary Society," in *The Thought of Paul Tillich* (ed. James Luther Adams, Wilhelm Pauck, and Roger Lincoln Shinn; San Francisco: Harper & Row, 1985), 343.

63. Dietrich Bonhoeffer, *Sanctorum Communio: A Theological Study of the Sociology of the Church* (vol. 1 of *Dietrich Bonhoeffer Works*; trans. Reinhard Krauss and Nancy Lukens; English ed. Clifford Green; Minneapolis, MN: Fortress, 1998). Hereafter referred to as *Sanctorum Communio*.

64. Ibid., 125.

65. Ibid., 145.

66. Ibid., 158.

67. Ibid., 189.

68. Ibid., 224.

69. *The New Oxford Annotated Bible* (New Revised Standard Version; New York: Oxford University Press, 1991), OT, 943.

70. Bonhoeffer, *Sanctorum Communio*, 236.

71. Ibid., 243.

72. Ibid., 252.

73. Ibid., 257.

74. Ibid., 280.

75. Ibid., 287.

76. Ibid.

77. Dietrich Bonhoeffer, *Discipleship* (vol. 4 of *Dietrich Bonhoeffer Works*; trans. Barbara Green and Reinhard Krauss; English ed. Geffrey B. Kelly and John D. Godsey; Minneapolis, MN: Fortress, 2001).

78. Ibid., 215.

79. Ibid., 218.

80. Dietrich Bonhoeffer, *Letters and Papers from Prison* (enl. ed., incorporates text from the 1970 3d ed.; ed. Eberhard Bethge; New York: Collier, 1972), 279–81.

4

RECENT VIEWS OF TRADITIONAL CATHOLIC ECCLESIOLOGY

Yves Congar (1904–95)

It can be said that Yves Congar dedicated his long life to the study of the church. He did his theology at the Institut Catholique in Paris; in 1931 he was appointed professor of theology at Saulchoir, the Dominican house of studies in Paris. Congar taught at Saulchoir most of his life. His first book, *Divided Christendom*, was published in 1937. As a result of an article written in defense of the priest-worker movement, he was removed from his teaching post in 1954. His fortunes changed with Pope John XXIII, who appointed him as a theological consultant to the preparatory commission doing the initial work for Vatican II. Congar was a very important contributor to the *Constitution on Divine Revelation*, the *Constitution on the Church*, and the *Decree on Ecumenism*. During his last active years, he worked at the Convent Saint-Jacques in Paris. In 1984, due to a paralyzing illness, he was moved to the Hotel des Invalides, where he remained until his death in 1995.

His *Divided Christendom* appeared in English in 1939.[1] Congar traces the division between the East and the West from the seventh century, at which time Constantinople began to call itself the Ecumenical (or Universal) Patriarchate, thus implicitly denying the primacy of the pope in Rome. A *modus vivendi* of sorts between the East and West existed until the eleventh century, when the estrangement became more severe. After the fall of Constantinople in 1453, the heritage of the Christian empire passed to Russia, and Moscow assumed the title of the third Rome. The Greeks from the beginning had little interest in ecclesiology and manifested only modest concern regarding the church's institutional structure.

Concerning the West, Congar outlines the erosion of confidence in the church after the eleventh century. The separations in the sixteenth century have remained and, in fact, increased over the following centuries. The rigorous Catholic response resulted in a hardening of the lines of difference, and the steady increase of centralization effected by the pope and the papal curia brought more authority than ever before into Rome. The stiffening of attitudes between the Reformers and the Catholic Church became a further obstacle to the possibility of reconciliation or reunion. "The Roman primacy has thus developed its mode of exercise on the sociological side, in the judicial and administrative sphere, by establishing a régime characterized by frequent intervention from the center."[2] There has been quite diverse doctrinal development among Catholics and Protestants. Whereas Congar feels that Catholics have placed a heavy emphasis on the juridical and institutional dimension, the Reformers have taken much less interest in these issues. Actually, Protestant theology has deemphasized the juridical. The Catholic situation was rendered even more rigid at Vatican I (1869–70) when the chapter on the powers and prerogatives of the papacy turned out to be the only jurisdictional area in the church to be formally and fully treated and defined.

Although in the East even as late as the nineteenth century it was possible for Roman Catholic priests to exercise their ministry in Orthodox churches, the deep differences in mentality between East and West remain unchanged. In the West, the deep divide regarding Luther's notions of justification and Calvin's understanding of predestination persists. Congar urges us to keep in mind the ideal of the organic unity of the church whose function is to manifest the presence of the kingdom of God in the world. The church's mission is to proclaim, from one end of the earth to the other, all the truths revealed by Christ with as clear a voice as possible. Furthermore, according to Congar, the church is to adapt itself to the many different segments of the human family so that the message of the gospel of Jesus can be heard and understood everywhere.

Congar notes that the Church of England is somewhat different from the other Protestant communities in that it has retained some of the externals of worship as well as the ecclesiastical hierarchy.[3] The Church of England claims to be a Christian church but does not identify itself as *the* true church. This so-called branch theory was devised by a number of theologians in the Oxford movement in the nineteenth century. According to this group, no one church represents the church of Christ completely. They hold that the catholic church visibly exists in various groups of churches, but its total unity has not yet been achieved.[4] For Congar, this understanding of the church as a federation of churches is not an acceptable expression of the church's unity.

Between the Orthodox and the Roman Catholics, the only crucial difference of opinion has to do with the primacy, which is not acknowledged in the East as the supreme ecclesiastical authority. The Orthodox insist that the church is not to be thought of in primarily juridical and institutional categories, but rather as a living fellowship of faith, hope, and charity.

Rather than emphasizing the juridical dimension, Orthodox scholars over the centuries have been more inclined to feature the body of Christian believers in terms that are more appropriate to the church triumphant. In Congar's view, children baptized in the separated churches, Protestant or Orthodox, do become to some degree genuine members of the true church of Christ. And furthermore:

> Insofar as particular dissident Christian bodies have preserved some or other of the means which God has ordained to unite men with Himself and imparted to His Christ and His Church, they are, in spite of error, in possession of something which belongs to the nature and integrity of the one Church, some fibers of her very being. In the measure, therefore, in which *in* these communities and *by* their officials, the true Word of God is preached and His sacraments administered to them, the souls who belong to them may truly be said to be sanctified *in* these bodies and even *by* them.[5]

In our day, Congar's position sounds very ordinary, but in 1939, it was rather new.

In 1941, Congar published *The Mystery of the Church*, which appeared in English in 1960.[6] Christ is identified as the second Adam and the head of the new order of things that is the church.[7] The reception of baptism brings us all into a single body, while the Eucharist allows us to participate more deeply in Christ's fellowship and his life. The various sacraments bring about our oneness with Christ. Acts 2:41–47 reflects clearly the life and activity of the primitive church. As a society of humans, the church must have a certain orderly distribution of powers and functions. Congar identifies the pastoral power of governing, the sacerdotal power of sanctifying, and the prophetic power of teaching. He declares that these functions proceed from Christ "according to a law of hierarchical procession."[8] Over the centuries, the church has taken to itself a considerable variety of external shapes that have not always been irreproachable, and which frequently only remotely resemble the primitive structures. Congar notes that the treatise on the church has been formulated often in the most adverse of circumstances, and thus it unfortunately reflects a heavy emphasis on its hierarchical constitution, the primacy of Peter, and the subordination of all dioceses and churches to the will and direction of the Roman See.

Congar follows Aquinas in describing the church as the congregation of the faithful from the time of Abel to the end of time. It is the existing form of the mystical body.[9] The sacraments and the ministry give visible shape to the church, which was established by Christ and propagated by the apostles. According to Congar, Thomas Aquinas charted a fairly developed theology of the church at the end of the *Secunda Pars* of the *Summa Theologica*. The whole church is portrayed by Aquinas as a great sacrament whose soul is the Eucharist, "whence flow and whither tend all the other sacraments and sacramentals, powers and ministries."[10]

In the course of actually becoming universal in its mission, the church became aware of its universality. The Holy Spirit inspired this universalism. Congar also affirms that the primacy of the Holy See became clear only after many generations. Pope Callistus (217–22) was the first to cite Matthew 16:18 as the precedent for papal primatial power. The sacraments developed in roughly the same fashion. A ritual like the anointing of the sick came through the years to be seen as a privileged action of the church with special saving effects. "[P]recisely because it is an institution and not just a dogma, more can be learned about it by watching it live than by studying its formula."[11]

In the first century of the church, the two operative agents were the Holy Spirit and the apostles. The apostolic office was given its configuration by Christ (Matt 18:18; Luke 22:19; John 13:16, 19). The mission of the Holy Spirit was portrayed as a distinct and separate function. The Spirit is "another Paraclete," whose mission is to bring to mind and to clarify all that Christ had spoken to them (John 14:26). In Congar's view, Christ has established the gifts of grace and truth, and the Holy Spirit is to implant these gifts within each person and bring about his or her growth and maturation (John 16:13). With the Orthodox, we consistently find a strong emphasis on the Spirit, which stands in opposition to the heavy Catholic stress on authority and legalism.

When the apostles completed their mission, they surrendered their role, leaving Christ and the Holy Spirit to inspire the course of the community. According to Congar, the church derives its very structure from the inspiration of the apostles, the life of the sacraments, and the deposit of faith. At Pentecost, the church was established as a new creation with its own specific energies.[12] Tradition has bestowed on the Holy Spirit the designation as the soul of the church, for the Spirit gives life and direction to the community, as well as to the apostolic ministry: "Whatever be the terms employed, it remains that the certainty of God's promise and the covenant bond existing between the Church and the Holy Spirit are the ground of the infallibility of the hierarchical actions, of those, that is, by which the visible Church visibly builds its structure and is linked, by the visible bond of apostolicity to Christ's institution."[13]

The Spirit dispenses the life-giving charisms (see Rom 12) that were later made subject to the apostolic authority. However, the *charismata* in the majority of instances do not flow from the activity of the hierarchy, but rise up from below. Congar is consistently opposed to any description of the church as simply one organization among many organizations in the world. For him, the charismatic and the spiritual must always keep the institutional in proper balance. Although the Holy Spirit is a distinct person with a specific mission, the Spirit "will not speak on his own, but he will speak whatever he hears, and he will declare to you the things that are to come" (John 16:13). The Holy Spirit "will teach you everything, and remind you of all that I have said to you" (John 14:26).

At Pentecost, the church came into being and received its animating principle, the Holy Spirit.

> The Lord had instituted the elements which were to make up the Church in the course of his public life. He instituted the apostolic office and made choice of the Twelve, giving the primacy to Peter. He made known the mystery of God as proclaimed in the Gospel; he instituted the sacraments. Thus, gradually the structure of the Church was built up. Then, at the end of the paschal fifty days, he gave it its living principle, the Holy Spirit.[14]

In the Acts of the Apostles, the church was established through the hierarchical functions of preaching, the celebration of the sacraments, and spiritual governance. Congar teaches that definitive doctrinal decisions are to involve the unanimous affirmation of the body of bishops gathered around Peter.[15] Such decisions, he feels, have the value of God's own witness.

Congar's *Power and Poverty in the Church*, published during the Second Vatican Council, outlines the major developments in the church's patterns of authority from the age of the martyrs to the twentieth century.[16] The bond with the believing community has been essential from the earliest years. There is little doubt that in the first centuries the spiritual or mystical and the juridical elements were much more closely related. Also, the laity and the bishops were not as distanced from one another as in more recent times. Congar quotes the African bishop Cyprian of Carthage (d. 258) in this connection: "I have made it a rule, ever since the beginning of my episcopate, to make no decision merely on the strength of my own personal opinion without consulting you (the priests and the deacons), without the approbation of the people."[17] Then Congar adds the following, "In fact the whole church community, the laity especially, took part in the election of bishops and the choice of ministers."[18]

From Constantine (d. 337) to Pope Gregory VII (1073–85), there were many less than favorable developments in Christian society. The clergy acquired significant privileges that separated them from the lay people.

Charismatic authority, which in earlier times was often found together with the authority of bishops, now more often found its way into monastic life. Although there were a good number of bishops noted for their spirituality (Ambrose, Augustine, Gregory), prelates in the church came to be more often identified as territorial lords and members of the aristocratic class.

After the fourth and fifth centuries, the clergy obtained important immunities from the secular authorities, while a special garb was introduced to set off the clergy from the rest of society. Despite the fact that Pope Celestine I (422–32) spoke out against such distinctive clerical dress, this failed to stop the trend. The practice of celibacy, which began to be introduced in this period, further separated the clergy from the lay people. Congar stresses that the church came to be governed more and more by a clerical caste of men who appeared to be part of the *illustri*, the noble class.

The pontificates of Leo IX (1048–54) and Gregory VII (1073–85) constituted an unmistakable turning point regarding the exercise of ecclesiastical authority. In his *Dictatus Papae* (1075), Gregory outlined a bold system of rights and prerogatives especially for the Roman See. He fearlessly assumed power over kings and princes and encouraged canonical scholars to corroborate his position. The papal power was to be supreme over all and could be judged and overruled by no one. This political posture was strengthened by a succession of popes such as Innocent III (1198–1216), and it reached a high-water mark with Boniface VIII (1294–1303).

In many church documents of the time, the church came to be identified as a clerical system centered in the hierarchy and ultimately in the Roman curia. As Congar puts it: "It is a fact that 'Church' is sometimes understood by the theorists of ecclesiastical power or papal authority as indicating clerics, priests and the pope. This use of the word was completely unknown to the Fathers and the liturgy. It is a fact that in a large number of modern documents, the word 'Church' indicates the priestly government or even quite simply this government's Roman courts."[19] Congar notes that this change of meaning is in no way consonant with the evidence in Scripture and in the Fathers of the church. Furthermore,

> It cannot be denied that, from the eleventh century onwards, authority and in particular the supreme authority of the pope, borrowed many of the features of the vocabulary, insignia, ceremonial, style and ideology of the imperial court. . . . Even the title of *Curia* assumed by the papal administration was borrowed from the secular vocabulary and, at the time, there were those who did not fail to point this out.[20]

Congar affirms that this change of meaning is in no way consonant with the earliest traditions, and he adds that these modifications are out of keeping with the patterns found in the primitive church.

Congar then briefly reviews the period from the Council of Trent (1545–63) to the present. He points out that whenever the church has been seriously challenged, a greater emphasis on centralization has occurred, along with a tightening in the exercise of authority.

> The Church's reaction became clear from the time of the Council of Trent onwards. It consisted in the twofold process which the Church normally brings into operation when she is seriously challenged. On the one hand, she reasserted her authority and gave it a greater degree of centralization. On the other hand, she revised the idea and practice of authority on the moral and pastoral planes.[21]

Since the sixteenth century, there has been an even closer identification of God's will with the institutional and hierarchical practice of authority, resulting in a heavy emphasis on juridical elements. Congar reminds us that today we are living in a world where a more egalitarian spirit, along with the notion of the brotherhood of all the faithful, prevails. Christian authority in the New Testament is consistently presented in terms of service to others. However, in the age of Gregory VII and Boniface VIII, gospel texts had been used to justify what Congar terms "flagrant examples of the arrogant use of power."[22] He summarizes his views of papal and curial authority as follows:

> Has the Church likewise reviewed the profane elements, imperial, feudal or courtly, which for so long she not only tolerated but actively encouraged? The Holy Roman Empire no longer exists, but there still remain in the Church many titles and insignia, many elements of ceremonial and so of her visible aspect, borrowed at some time from the dazzling imperial splendour. Surely it is high time and surely it would be to everyone's advantage, 'to shake off the dust of the Empire that has gathered since Constantine's day on the throne of St. Peter.' Those words were spoken by John XXIII.[23]

One of Yves Congar's most important contributions to Catholic ecclesiology is his masterful study *Lay People in the Church*, published in French in 1953, with the English edition appearing in 1957.[24] He mentions in the introduction that by consistently defining the laity in relation to the clergy, we have hardened the distinction between them. Congar agrees with Karl Rahner in defining the lay Christian as one "whose Christian existence and responsibilities are determined by his native involvement in the life and organization of the world."[25] The church is to be seen primarily as the community of the faithful, while the hierarchy is to be understood as a function of service rather than as an authority. Yet even as late as the first decade of the twentieth century, Pope Pius X (1903–14), in his encyclical *Vehementer nos* of February 1906, addressed to the clergy and people of France, had this to say regarding the role of lay people in the church:

> It follows that the Church is essentially an unequal society, that is, a society comprising two categories of persons, the pastors and the flock, those who occupy a rank in the different degrees of the hierarchy and the multitude of the faithful. So distinct are these categories that with the pastoral body only rests the necessary right and authority for promoting the end of the society and directing all its members to that end; the one duty of the multitude is to allow themselves to be led, and like a docile flock, to follow the pastors.[26]

Pope Pius XI (1922–39) defined Catholic action as the participation of the laity in the hierarchical apostolate.[27] However, it was not until Vatican II's *Decree on the Laity* (1965) that the distinctive and inalienable mission of the laity vis-à-vis the Christianization of the human family and the world is charted out. Yves Congar's *Lay People in the Church* represents a critical stage in this important development.

Hans Küng (1928–)

Hans Küng was born in the quiet town of Sursee, Switzerland, in 1928. After studying philosophy and theology at the German College in Rome from 1948 to 1955, he obtained a doctorate in theology from the Institut Catholique in Paris in 1957. In 1960, he accepted a professorship at the University of Tübingen, where he remains even after his retirement from the theological faculty. His work, *The Council, Reform and Reunion*, published just before the opening of Vatican II, established his reputation throughout the Catholic world. Pope John XXIII appointed him as a specialist, a *peritus*, to the council.

Küng's *Structures of the Church*, published in 1962, was an effort to expand the current understanding of ecumenical councils just prior to Vatican II. He points out that there was a pervasive impression among

Catholic scholars, especially those trained in Rome, that the time of councils had passed, since the infallibility of the pope in matters of faith and morals had been solemnly defined at Vatican I (1870). Küng insists, however, that conciliar history remains an indispensable element of the church's life and must be emphasized, because the first seven councils are the key to the ultimate reunion between the East and the West.

Küng identifies the church as the great council of the faithful convoked by the Spirit, and he views the ecumenical council as the most authentic representation of the whole church. The unity of the church is aptly described by Paul in Ephesians 4:3–6 as one body and having one Spirit, one Lord, one baptism, one God and Father of all. Although the twenty-one ecumenical councils are described as perhaps the most significant events in the history of the church, Küng points to two universal councils as being essentially failures—Vienne (1311–12) and Lateran V (1512–17). He also notes that the much-debated and maligned Council of Constance (1414–18) was the only ecumenical council that was able to restore unity to the church.

Lay representation at the great councils was in varying degrees significant during the centuries up to Vatican I (1870), in which lay participation was almost nonexistent.[28] Although Martin Luther emphasized the universal priesthood of all, not until Pius XII (1939–58) was the importance of the laity restated for Catholics. In fact, in 1946, this pontiff said of them, "They are the church."[29] Both Luther and Calvin objected to the formal declarations of the councils being placed on or near the same plane as the Word of God. Despite the fact that in his early writings Martin Luther made little provision for bishops, later he was most favorable toward these officials; he felt that they are to establish order among the priests. He reminded his followers that Titus, Timothy, Paul, and Barnabas presided over the installation of priests.

After the death of the apostles, the function of leadership was carried on through the pastoral office. The Council of Trent (1545–63) adopted a strong position on the transmission of powers and offices through the rite of ordination and considered this transmission of divine right. Küng is certain that the papal office remains the major obstacle for the Protestants and the Orthodox on the road to reunion with Rome. He affirms, "The rigidity of the Roman Catholic Church since the Reformation has made it difficult for Protestant Christians to see the justification of the papacy as such."[30] According to Küng, the papal office must be limited to its status in the New Testament and in the early traditions. The towering figure of the pope in the last several centuries has reduced and diminished the situation of the bishops in the church, such that one occasionally wonders whether the bishops are nothing more than spokesmen and representatives of the pope. "The Petrine office therefore may never, like a totalitarian state, lay claim to attending to everything, or at least to being empowered by law to attend to everything. This would be a fateful misunderstanding of the Vatican [Vatican I] definitions."[31]

The reduction or limitation of papal power is indispensable for the full restoration of the episcopal office as it existed and operated in the first one thousand years. Küng insists that the primacy of the pope and his infallibility as defined by Vatican I have been vehemently rejected by the overwhelming majority of non-Catholics. According to Pope Pius XII, the principle of subsidiarity is also valid for the life of the church as long as it does not violate the church's hierarchical structure. Küng articulates the principle: "What the individual can accomplish on his [her] own power should not be done by the community, and what the subordinated community accomplishes should not be done by the superordinated community. The community must respect the individual, the superordinated [higher] community, the subordinated community [the lower community]."[32]

It is clearly, then, a violation of right order for a higher organization to take unto itself functions that can be performed effectively by smaller and lower bodies. Although some Catholic theologians in recent times have seriously questioned the applicability of the principle of subsidiarity to the church, this principle can be considered in the great majority of cases as perfectly justifiable when applied to the church and its organization. The establishment of the order of bishops as set forth in the New Testament must be given its due place in the church. Relegating them to the position of mere delegates of the pope is a violation of the divine order recognized from apostolic times: "Even John Paul II in his 1995 encyclical, *Ut unum sint*, has admitted that the current structure and exercise of the papal role is an obstacle to Christian reunion, and he has acknowledged his responsibility to give the office a new shape and a new situation."[33]

The Council of Constance represents for Küng a true watershed in the constitutional development of the church. Its decree *Haec sancta* (April 1415) declares that a legitimately assembled council has its authority immediately from Christ and that everyone, including the pope, is bound to obey it in matters that pertain to the faith, the eradication of schism, and also to the general reform of the church.[34] Two years later (October 1417), the council, through its decree *Frequens*, directed that ecumenical councils should be held henceforth at fixed intervals, preferably every ten years, in perpetuity.[35] Because of the profound confusion inflicted on the church by the Western Schism (1378–1415), which had given the church three simultaneously reigning pontiffs, a period of indescribable chaos had ensued. The rather sudden restoration of the absolute papacy under Martin V (1417–31) and Eugene IV (1431–47) precipitated an almost immediate reaction to the decrees of 1415 and 1417, so that subsequent centuries were inclined to consider them either invalid or of merely temporary applicability. Küng insists, however, that the two decrees are "almost undisputedly conciliar," and carry (at least with regard to *Haec sancta*) permanent and lasting force.[36]

Pope Pius II (1458–64) forbade any appeal from the dictates of the pope to an ecumenical council. This prohibition was reaffirmed in the nineteenth century by Vatican I. John XXIII was the pontiff who once again brought the idea of the importance of ecumenical councils to the attention of the world. The noted churchman Nicholas of Cusa (1401–64) turned from being an advocate of moderate conciliarism, which he professed in his *De Concordantia Catholica* (1433?), to monarchical papalism several years later. He is still considered, however, one of the foremost conciliar theorists.

In 1967, two years after Vatican II, Küng's treatise on the church was published in German and appeared in English in the same year.[37] This study has been widely used, at least in the English-speaking world, as a textbook in ecclesiology for more than a generation. According to Küng, there is no historical evidence that Jesus intended his gospel to be preached to the Gentiles. Yet when he spoke eschatologically, he seemed to include everyone in his good news of salvation. Paul developed the notion that the gospel is destined for both Jews and Gentiles. In the Letter to the Romans, he discusses the relationship between Israel and the church, which is to include both Jews and Gentiles. The designation of the church as a chosen race and God's own people in 1 Peter 2:9–10 is a dramatic application of the notion "people of God" to the New Testament church.

Küng stresses again and again that the church must not be clericalized.[38] He attests that not until the third century did a clear distinction between clerics and lay people appear. Further, the church must always see itself as "on the way," a church *semper reformanda*. In spite of the church's rather unfortunate history of anti-Semitism, the Jews are always to be regarded as God's people. The promises made by God to Israel still remain in effect, for God's unambiguous aim is to bring Israel to salvation. The call issued by God to Israel remains irrevocable.

For Küng, the church has in many ways become a place of unfreedom. There is much sinfulness in the church, along with a growing spirit of legalism. Despite its many failures, the church always possesses the Spirit of God. Over the past seven or eight centuries, the charismatic structure of the church has been frequently overlooked. Juridical thinking along with a legalistic mindset have on many occasions frustrated the movements of the Spirit. The ecclesiology of the Catholic textbooks over the past two to three hundred years has been based largely on the Pastoral Epistles rather than on the charismatic spirit of Paul's notion of church. In a church where only the ecclesiastical officials are important and operative, one can ask to what extent the movements of the Spirit have been sacrificed or ignored.[39] In the Catholic Church since Trent (1545–63), the reading of sacred Scripture has become rather marginal, while more attention has been given to various devotions and novenas emphasizing the cult of the saints.

Baptism has been from the outset the rite of entrance into the believing community. Early on, it was conferred in the name of Jesus (Acts 2:38; 8:16). It was administered only once because of the radically new character which it bestowed. The oldest biblical version of the Lord's Supper is to be found in 1 Corinthians 11:23–26, dating probably from the mid-fifties. From the beginning, fellowship with Christ was demonstrated in a singular manner in the eucharistic meal, which recalls the death of Christ and anticipates the future kingdom of God. The early disciples were certain that the risen Jesus would be present among them in the breaking of the bread (Matt 18:20). They were convinced that partaking of the eucharistic bread made them one body (1 Cor 10:17).

In Paul's writings, the body of Christ is the individual community in 1 Corinthians and Romans, while in Colossians and Ephesians, the body of Christ represents the whole church. According to Küng, tradition replaced the Scriptures as the prevailing source of Christian truth at Trent, while at Vatican I, the historical tradition took second place to the current teachings of the church's magisterium. The properties of the church—unity, holiness, catholicity, and apostolicity—are not only gifts but tasks to be accomplished in every succeeding age. The failures of the Catholic Church in the last two or three centuries—the increasing exercise of the centralization of authority in the Vatican, the corresponding weakening of the status and vitality of the local and regional churches—have made the task of reunion of all Christian churches far more daunting. There is also a reasonable share of guilt on the part of the other Christian bodies that have continued to become more and more fragmented, thus dissipating the force of the church vis-à-vis the non-Christian world. Vatican II (1962–65) formally recognized the existence and the character of the Christian bodies outside the Catholic communion. According to Küng, "we can apply the name Church to any community of baptized Christians modeled on Holy Scripture, who believe in Christ the Lord, wish to celebrate the Lord's Supper, try to live according to the Gospel, and wish to have the name of Church."[40]

Küng notes that the early church was by no means a uniform group. In fact, there was an extremely wide range of diverse expressions in theory and in practice. Nonetheless, by 380 or so, the Catholic Church became the only lawful religion in the Roman Empire. Since the separation of the East and the West, and after the Reformation in the West, each Christian church owes part of its reality to its relationship with this one church.[41] In Küng's judgment, the Catholic Church is in some sense the mother of the others. The notion of church can be applied to all the Christian bodies who are communities of the baptized and who are united in the profession of the New Testament.

In the past eight hundred years, the Catholic Church has become increasingly narrow; more recently, it has failed to adapt to the worlds of Asia and Africa. However, the church can be considered holy to the extent that it accepts the call to the Lord's service by being sent into the world to preach the Good News. The holiness of the church is the work of the Holy Spirit and is not per se controllable by the members. Küng affirms that the whole church possesses the authority to forgive sins because Matthew 18:18 is addressed to the whole community of the disciples.[42] In this context, the author raises the question of the general absolution of sins and of the possibility of absolution by lay believers. Furthermore, for Küng, there is no doubt that the church will remain until the end of time, for the powers of death shall not prevail against it (Matt 16:18).

The original meaning of the term "apostolic" when applied to the church refers to the direct link that the believing community has with the apostles and hence with the earthly Jesus. In the first century, there was a certain reluctance to undertake a mission to the Gentiles, and it was said only of Peter that he among the apostles left Jerusalem and traveled elsewhere (Acts 12:17). The missionary journeys that we usually hear about are those of Paul and Barnabas. The twelve apostles are indeed the fundamental witnesses of Christ's resurrection. After the martyrdom of James, the brother of John the evangelist, there was no attempt to replace him, and thus the college of the Twelve eventually died out. The continuity of the apostles then consisted in the agreement between the One sent and the apostolic witness, which is handed down in the New Testament. These writings were accepted by the church as the authentic testimony of the apostolic message.[43]

Neither Jesus nor any one of the Twelve is described in the Gospels as a priest. The apostolic proclamations more closely resembled the Old Testament prophetic utterances. However, it is in his passion and death that Christ reveals his priesthood, and thus he is referred to as a mediator in the later New Testament writings. Küng insists that all believers are called to hear and proclaim the Word. In the early centuries, lay preaching was rather common, but soon the function of proclamation was restricted to the officeholders. The tension between the church and the world in some respects shifted gradually to a tension between the clergy and the laity.

Küng attests that the most important New Testament ministries are preaching and reconciling. Paul speaks of apostles, prophets, and teachers (1 Cor 12:28). The prophets light the way to the present and the future, while the teachers ground their message in the testimony of the apostles. In the second century, there were still individuals called prophets, but they seemed to disappear in the third century.[44] Bishops first became visible in the Greek Christian communities, although there often were several officials called bishops in a number of the early churches. Deacons also seem to have appeared in the Greek-speaking locations. Küng asserts that there appeared to be neither a monarchical episcopate nor special ordination ceremonies in Paul's communities. Luke's observation that Paul and Barnabas appointed elders in every church is not borne out in the authentic Pauline letters.[45] Also, the letters of Paul contain a rather consistent identification of the titles "bishop" and "presbyter."

Bishops gradually became the sole leaders of the communities and came to be especially revered as the successors of the apostles. It seems that the monarchical episcopate was originally developed in Asia Minor and Syria. Regional synods of bishops began to convene in the early second century, while in the fourth century, the bishops of Rome, Alexandria, Antioch, and Constantinople were awarded the rank of metropolitans. After Küng briefly summarizes the institutional development of the first several centuries, he affirms:

> Nothing is to be gained from concealing the fact which the brief sketch above makes amply clear, that a frightening gulf separates the Church of today from the original constitution of the Church. At the same time, the Church of the present must be able to justify itself too, in the light of its own origins—and especially in this respect, since it is here that the decisive differences between individual Christian Churches are to be found.[46]

As the appointed ministers became more prominent and the charismatic ministries became less evident, Küng observes that after the apostles left the field, the charismatic ministries came more and more under the control of the ordained ministers. In the latter first century and early second century, the charismatic structure of the church gave way to a hierarchy of pastors. The loss of the prophetic voices in the church after the first several generations gave way to the controlling influence of the ordained ministers. Although they did not form a class apart in terms of their dress and lifestyle, the pastors were essential to the governance of the Christian communities and served as the ordinary ministers of the sacraments and worship. Küng defines the role of the pastors: "He [the pastoral minister] has power to found and to govern communities, to call together, unite and build up the community; he has power to preach the word in the public assembly and to carry it out into the world as a missionary; he has power to lead public assemblies, to baptize and celebrate the Lord's Supper, to bind and to loose and to commission others like himself."[47]

Regarding the Petrine ministry, Küng attests that more and more the church has come under the total and absolute authority of the pope in the West. He insists that the centralized system of papal government, which has increased dramatically since the thirteenth century, is the principal reason for the schism between East and West. In fact, "There is no way round the depressing conclusion that the development of this centralized Church with absolutist means was only achieved at the cost of dividing Christendom."[48] The papacy must always be limited by the existence and integrity of the episcopate, which must never be rendered impotent by the monarchical absolutism of the bishop of Rome. Küng reminds his readers that at least from the 1300s to the Council of Trent, an ecumenical council was considered by the great majority of theologians as superior to the authority of the pope alone. In fact, this position was maintained by certain significant theologians until Vatican I (1870).

Although Peter is not mentioned again after his discussion with the others regarding the church's mission to the Gentiles (Acts 15:7), there is continuing interest in him in the later New Testament writings. The Roman claim to primacy had been clearly articulated in the West by the time of Pope Leo I (440–61). Since Gregory VII (1073–85), the papacy has adopted a rather consistently imperial tone. In conclusion, Hans Küng asks whether there is a way back from the primacy of dominion to the primacy of service, and whether the new direction of Pope John XXIII (1958–63) will have a lasting effect. The answer to these two questions forty years after Vatican II seems to be in the negative.

In 1994, Hans Küng published his *Christianity: Essence, History, and Future* to address what he terms a massive crisis in Christendom, which is experiencing serious losses in membership across Europe and the Western church.[49] The failure to make the adjustments required by contemporary society and culture has brought the traditional churches to their knees, and Küng insists that these bodies must engage in a vigorous program of reform and renewal so that the authentic Christian message and practice might be revived. He defines the Christian church as a community of those who believe in Christ.[50] Küng calls for a thorough evaluation of the doctrine of the Trinity and asks, "Where does this doctrine really come from?"[51] The New Testament lifts the risen Christ to the right hand of

God and speaks of the Spirit as the representative of the risen Christ on earth, but the formulation of the doctrine in the early ecumenical councils carried us somewhat beyond the New Testament evidence.

Küng reminds us that in the Pauline literature and Acts, women were among the most prominent members of the churches. Of the twenty-nine significant persons addressed in Romans (16:1–16), ten were women. The absence of this kind of feminine presence in the present church calls for dramatic changes. Since the second century, women have been losing ground in the Christian community.[52] With the division of the Roman Empire under Theodosius in 395, the cultures of the East and the West began to drift apart. The population of Constantinople under Justinian I (527–65) amounted to more than three hundred thousand inhabitants, while Rome in the sixth century had a population of no more than twenty thousand.

The East and the West came to understand each other less and less in the second half of the first millennium. The papal claims of supreme and unconditional authority over the whole church from the time of Pope Gelasius I (492–96) to Gregory VII (1073–85) progressively alienated the East. The twin excommunications of Cardinal Humbert and Bishop Cerularius in 1054 deepened the division, while the Crusades, especially the Fourth Crusade in 1204, marked the beginning of the end.[53] After the fall of Constantinople in 1453, Moscow became the new center of orthodoxy in the East, and in the fifteenth century, the Russian church claimed its own head. During the long reign of Peter the Great (1672–1725) the state became an absolute authority over the church.[54] Küng notes that the state-church system remains a continuing danger to the Orthodox Church.

In the West, the aspirations of the popes for greater authority and influence were finally realized with Pope Innocent III (1198–1216), when the long-asserted claims and the actual possession of such power coincided. In Küng's judgment, the prohibition of marriage for the clergy further divided them from the faithful. As the papal influence increased in the West, it came into continued conflict with long-standing episcopal rights and prerogatives, which were decidedly weakened by the repeated incursions of Rome. The movement of the papal court from Rome to Avignon (1309–77) and the multiple financial excesses of that period did much to erode the credibility of the pope and his court throughout Christendom. After the Council of Constance (1414–18), which healed the Great Western Schism, papal absolutism asserted itself again under the Renaissance pontiffs of the fifteenth century. By 1500, the Christian world was clamoring for a reform council that would abolish the many abuses flowing from the pope's court and reform the church "in head and members." It was clear that the fifteenth-century popes were unable and even in many cases unwilling to address the many ills of the church in the West.

The Council of Trent (1545–63) addressed the doctrinal problems raised by the Reformers, but in the process, the power and influence of the papal curia continued to expand to the disadvantage of local and regional organs of ecclesiastical government. In the nineteenth century, the church took an extremely reactionary turn. "From the beginning, Counter-Reformation Rome was against modern philosophy, against modern science, against the modern theory of the state and of course also against the slogan 'Freedom, Equality, Brotherhood.'"[55] Pius IX (1846–78) became an unrelenting reactionary against liberalism of all sorts. His *Syllabus of Errors* (1864), in Küng's words, "represented the absolutely uncompromising defense of the mediaeval Counter-Reformation structure of doctrine and power, and moreover was regarded everywhere as a general declaration of war against the paradigm of modernity."[56] In Vatican I (1870), the pope was solemnly declared infallible in matters of faith and morals; then, in 1907, Pius X condemned modernism in all its forms and shapes.

A concluding note regarding Küng's attempts at explaining papal infallibility:

The publication of Pope Paul VI's encyclical *Humanae vitae* in 1968 constituted a watershed in Küng's career. His views regarding papal infallibility initiated a debate between Küng and the Doctrinal Congregation in Rome, which continued during the 1970s. He was eventually stripped of his canonical mission to teach as a Catholic theologian in December 1979.

Pope Paul's rejection of all artificial methods of birth control in 1968 shook the credibility of the papal teaching office throughout the Catholic world. Küng's *Infallible? An Inquiry* was published in German in 1970, and appeared in English in 1971.[57] In the study, Küng enumerates the more significant errors of the church's teaching office over the centuries, including the ban on lending money, the condemnation of Galileo, the condemnation of the new methods of critical exegesis of the Bible, and the attack against modernism. He then analyzes in detail the teaching of *Humanae vitae*, which condemns all artificial methods of birth control as forbidden by the natural law. Paul VI could not contradict the teaching of Pope Pius XI in 1930 (*Casti connubii*), for this dramatic reversal of opinion would mean that the church had been in error in a significant area of morality for more than a generation. Paul VI therefore simply reaffirmed the teaching of Pius XI against the advice of the episcopal commission he had employed to study this issue.

For Küng, the papal teaching on this issue affirmed by three popes over a period of more than a generation amounted to an exercise of the ordinary papal magisterium in a matter of no little importance—affecting the consciences of millions of Catholics. This kind of papal teaching would clearly amount to an exercise of the ordinary magisterium of the pope and hence be considered an exercise of the infallible teaching office. Because this moral teaching "had been specifically taught by bishops everywhere in the world, acting in moral unity and by common consent, as Catholic morality to be observed on pain of eternal damnation," it does constitute infallible Catholic teaching.[58]

Küng then asks whether the infallibility of the church really stands or falls on the existence of infallible propositions that have been judged by great numbers of the faithful over a considerable period of time to be in error. He responds: "The dilemma can be resolved only by raising the alternatives to a higher level and asserting that the church will remain in truth in spite of all the errors that are always possible."[59] Küng then proposes another interpretation of inerrancy and substitutes the term indefectibility for infallibility. The truth of the church "is not dependent on any fixed, infallible propositions, but on her remaining in the truth throughout all propositions, including erroneous ones."[60] The perpetuity of the church in truth is not substantially affected by occasional errors in detail. Although he affirms the position of infallibility, he prefers to call it indefectibility or perpetuity. This teaching of Küng has been much discussed and debated by theologians and is in need of further expansion, clarification, and correction.

Karl Rahner (1904–84)

Karl Rahner did his graduate studies at Freiburg in Germany and Innsbruck in Austria. After World War II, he returned to Innsbruck as a professor of theology. From 1964 to 1967 he taught at the University of Munich, and from 1967 to his retirement in 1971 he taught at the University of Münster. In the judgment of a great many scholars, Karl Rahner is considered the foremost Catholic theologian of the twentieth century. David Tracy of the University of Chicago has said that Rahner's *Foundations of Christian Faith* represents "the clearest and most systematic expression by Rahner of his own position."[61] Also, Rahner himself has said, "What is most important is contained more or less in my *Foundations of Christian Faith*."[62] This study was published in 1976 in

German and appeared in English in 1978. According to Rahner, the church is "the historical continuation of Christ in and through the community of those who believe in him, and who recognize him explicitly as the mediator of salvation in a profession of faith."[63] He considers the church as in no way accidental to humankind's essence. However, he does not understand the doctrine of the church to be at the very core of the ultimate truth of Christianity. In the hierarchy of truths, ecclesiology is not at the very center of Christianity.

Rahner maintains that the church can be considered as having something of a constitution with disciples and a mission at the time that Christ was raised from the dead. However, to trace the founding of the church back to Jesus, the acknowledgment of the primacy of Peter, and the doctrine of apostolic succession back to the earthly Jesus allows for some differences of opinion.[64] In the period of the New Testament, different notions of the church were held by various groups of believers. Could the earthly Jesus see what would come after the passing of his apostles? There were a great number of possibilities latent in the earliest church that were perhaps never fully realized. The Petrine office and the episcopal constitution of the first Christian communities were, according to Rahner, binding on successive generations.[65] The calling of the Twelve was in effect the claim he made upon the whole of Israel.

According to Rahner, Matthew 16:18–19 reveals Jesus' intention to found a church. Peter was to be the foundation stone of his community, and Christ guaranteed its survival against the powers of darkness. The power of binding and loosing was given to the Twelve, and thus the community of Jesus was given its basic constitution. The word "church" was given to the individual Jewish Christian communities, then to Paul's congregations, and finally to the whole church. There are indications of the theology of church in the Gospel of Matthew, and Paul's ecclesiology is not surpassed even today. The church composed of both Jews and pagans was established on baptism and the Eucharist. Paul developed, with considerable clarity, the notion of the church as the body of Christ.

In the Pastoral Epistles, we witness the church described as a well-organized house of God, with offices, ordination, and fixed teaching. First Peter 2:4–10 contains a memorable description of the priesthood of all believers. The Gospel and the letters of John emphasize the sacraments of baptism and the Lord's Supper and point to the church's future life. Rahner attests that the New Testament church was already fairly well-established institutionally.[66] Most of the elements of the constitution of the church were in place by the second and third centuries. One can therefore conclude that Christian faith and practice are not a purely private matter, because we are presented with a church that speaks to us and presides over religious practices, inviting all to take part. This Christian religious phenomenon is indeed a reality that God bestows on us.

Rahner affirms that the church of Christ is meant to be one church, and this is especially clear in the teachings of John and Paul. This church exists wherever baptism and the Eucharist are celebrated and wherever the Word of Christ is proclaimed. In Rahner's judgment, all true Christians share a common conviction that there should be one church.[67] Every Christian of good will may justly presume that his own ecclesial existence is legitimate and bestowed on him in the unfolding of history. Nonetheless, Rahner does assert that the closer the concrete historical connection between a given Christian church and the original Christian ecclesial experience, the greater the prospect that it is the true church of Christ.[68] The closer the continuity, the better. Rahner states that no Lutheran or Reformed Christian wants to make the claim that his or her church was not founded until the Reformation. A critical element is the historical continuity reaching all the way back to apostolic times. For Karl Rahner, Evangelical Christianity must affirm that a great deal in the pre-Reformation church is either superfluous or unchristian.[69] Catholic Christians, on the other hand, must not find anything so contrary in the church's previous history that it would force them to leave their church.

There is little doubt that Evangelical Christianity exerts a positive function for Catholicism, calling to mind that grace alone and faith alone are the true saving elements. Rahner sees the Scriptures as the church's book, and the New Testament as the objectification of the church of the apostolic age, which ended with the writing of the final New Testament books around the first decades of the second century. "[T]he church objectifies its faith and its life in written documents, and it recognizes these objectifications as so pure and so successful that they are able to hand on the apostolic church as a norm for future ages."[70]

The teaching office of the church does not take priority over Scripture but is to interpret it anew in the light of ever-changing historical horizons. It confronts us in ever-new concrete situations with the message of Jesus. "There is something like the teaching authority of the church within Evangelical Christianity too."[71] The difference, however, lies in the fact that such a thing as a binding declaration is rejected within the Evangelical church. Regarding the post-Tridentine development of dogma within Catholicism (for example, papal primacy and infallibility, the Immaculate Conception, and the Assumption of Mary), the church has been accused of creating new obstacles to unity among the churches. Rahner feels that it is always a great risk to have the pope in a position to make binding declarations on his own that will affect all Christians.[72] He does not argue that this power is inappropriate, but there are dangers, nonetheless. The Marian dogmas, although they constitute an added obstacle to the reunion of all Christians, are portrayed by Rahner as the result of the theological fact that Mary has been redeemed radically.

As a community, the church necessarily possesses a hierarchical structure, for a division of labor and functions is indispensable. Otherwise, the community would be nothing more than a disorganized gathering of religious individualists. Law and order are always critical for the life and vitality of the organization so that it might realize its goals. Rahner concludes with the observation that the church is to be thought of as the place where we have the assurance that God loves us.

Rahner's study *The Shape of the Church to Come*, which appeared in German in 1972, was composed in preparation for the German National Synod in 1971.[73] The role of the synod was to prepare the German Catholic Church to respond to the theology and the pastoral directives of Vatican II (1962–65). Rahner points out that the church in Germany is in transition from the status of a people's church or national church to a church made up of those individuals who have made an explicitly responsible decision leading them to personal membership. For Rahner, substantial changes have to be made in preparation for the future: "To win one new man of tomorrow for the faith is more important for the Church than to keep in the faith two men of yesterday; the latter will be saved by God's grace even if the present and future way of proclaiming the faith makes them insecure."[74]

The institutional church has more often than not favored conservative positions rather than more innovative ones, and this has been disadvantageous to progress and growth. The growing shortage of priests will force the closing of many parishes unless new candidates for ministry, married or single, are attracted to service. Rahner assures his readers that the role of the papacy may have to be structured in a different fashion to meet the needs of the modern world. "Often enough individual popes in the past 150 years have provided and still provide today an occasion for criticism even of the institution itself, and of what is claimed to be normal practice."[75] The decision-making process from the lowest to the highest levels in the church must involve the active participation of as many people as possible or feasible, and the proceedings should be visible to all.

The church must become desacralized, for the predominance of clerical voices frustrates and alienates many lay people. "[T]hose who love, who are unselfish, who have a prophetic gift in the Church, constitute the real Church and are far from being always identical with the office holders."[76] The church officials must be much more sensitive to the fact that the Spirit breathes where the Spirit wills. They must be made more aware that the charismatic element is just as necessary as the work of officials in the church. The pope, the bishops, and the Vatican bureaucracy have to be willing to reverse decisions that are counterproductive or harmful, because their mistakes in the past call for a more humble attitude in the future. In the area of moral pronouncements, officeholders must acknowledge that they do not always have all the answers. Furthermore, the church must take its stand more consistently on the side of the poor and the oppressed.

For Rahner, the church today is by no means clearly defined in terms of its membership; thus, open doors are necessary. He warns that we must be slow to judge that certain theological positions are unorthodox. In response to specific issues and the demand for clear directions for action, the church can declare itself not competent in this area, while individuals or groups with more specific expertise should be asked to devise answers for themselves based on general Christian principles. Rahner guards against "making too much use of a doctrinaire casuistry in proclaiming doctrine today."[77] Further, we must concentrate our efforts in taking an active part in the struggle for justice and freedom in society. "If we are honest we must admit that we are to a terrifying extent a spiritually life-less Church."[78] We are all too often dominated by ritualism, legalism, and administrative details. Rahner suggests that we have often repeated dogmatic formulas in the articulation of our faith that have become almost devoid of meaning for the people of the church.

It is no longer unchristian to ask whether the requirement of celibacy for priesthood should be put aside and whether women should be considered just as much as men for priestly offices in the church.[79] Also, it is not at all clear why divorced people who remarry should not be readmitted to the sacraments under certain conditions. Further, the Sunday mass obligation "cannot be pressed as if it had been proclaimed at Sinai as divine law, valid forever."[80] It has become ever-more challenging to set strict limits of orthodoxy for all church members in all circumstances. "In the light of this alone the Church is an open Church, whether she wants to be or not, whether she reflects on it or not, or simplifies the situation and thus overlooks it."[81]

Rahner then addresses the issue of ecumenism and the possible reunion of all Christians in light of the fact that the ecumenical movement seems to be stagnating. He suggests that we address the question of institutional unification first, rather than initially working to settle all the major theological issues.

> Hitherto (apart from improving relations and cooperating in social projects) we have tried to tackle the question of union from the theological and confessional aspect and regarded institutional

unification purely as a consequence of this settlement of contro-
versial theological issues. Would it not perhaps be possible to proceed in the opposite direction? Could we not consider full unity
of faith and theology as a consequence of institutional unification, particularly since the latter need not mean institutional uniformity based on dogma as hitherto envisaged by the Code of
Canon Law?[82]

Since there are in the Catholic Church—as in other Christian churches—
notable differences between the faith as formally preached and the faith as
professed by great numbers of people, it might be advisable first to unite
institutionally those churches that express their belief in Christ as God and
Savior and to leave the theological differences to be discussed and settled
by the theologians. This institutional approach to the unity of Christians
might well prove to be more effective. Rahner suggests that the papal office
could have as its principal function the maintenance of unity and the promotion of dialogue among the various member churches, which would
have, nevertheless, considerable autonomy concerning their belief systems.

Within the Catholic communion, base communities should be encouraged to emerge from below to complement territorial parishes. They could
unite for a number of reasons—professional, social, or a common interest
in the achievement of a special mission. The bond would not necessarily
be territorial, and these congregations would have the right to be recognized as true worshipping communities by their local bishop. In Rahner's
judgment, experimentation would bring forth and perfect the forms of
these communities, although he admits that his ideas here are quite vague
and sketchy.[83]

Rahner further urges that the appointment of officeholders in the
church be modified dramatically. There should be greater involvement
of those affected by the appointment. He suggests that both priests and
laity cooperate actively in the election of their bishops. Finally, he recommends that the church needs to be actively involved in more projects
that aim at the elimination of injustice in the world. These thoughts are
intended to complement Rahner's more formal ideas regarding the discipline of ecclesiology.

Leonardo Boff (1938–)

In connection with his book *The Church: Charism and Power*, published
in Portuguese in 1981 and translated into English in 1985, Leonardo Boff
was ordered to come to Rome to discuss a number of issues raised by the
study.[84] In spite of the intercession of two Brazilian cardinals on his behalf,

he was informed that he was to be silenced for a period of one year because of the dangers to sound doctrine in his notions concerning the Catholic Church. Boff submitted to this restriction but left the ministry; he petitioned for laicization in 1992.

For Boff, the church is always to be understood as a concrete sign of saving service to the world. The church has often allied itself with the dominant classes, the ruling classes. It is time now for the church to be identified with the poor. It has more often than not sided with the conservative elements, and its preaching has frequently lacked prophetic emphasis. Historically, the church has been comfortable with authoritative regimes, especially in Latin America. Many of the church's movements, for example, the charismatic renewal and the Christian Family Program, have gained adherents from people who have a somewhat comfortable situation in society.

Since the 1970s, especially in Latin America, a deepening sensitivity to the poor has developed. Boff is convinced that Central and South America have been stalled in terms of their economic development. They have in many cases been despoiled of their raw materials. He urges a reexamination of the capitalist system that has drained natural resources from Latin American countries, leaving them poor, while the capitalist nations, especially in North America, have become richer and richer. Current theology no longer speaks to Latin America because it does not deal with the deep and pervasive poverty that is so rampant there. The church must begin to speak more forcefully to the plight of the poor and the oppressed.

In Boff's judgment, traditional theology has been used as an instrument of domination over those who are technologically backward.[85] If the church has spent the last millennium as an agent of the established order, it is now gathering forces in order to be an agent of change and a force for the humanization of the world. The theological work of Jürgen Moltmann and Johannes B. Metz has been most instrumental in charting out the new signs of the times. As the poor of the third world countries are emerging as a social reality, the need for a theology of liberation becomes more and more urgent. Boff insists that God surely does not will this pervasive poverty. We must take part in the process of liberation, making use of nonviolent means. However, he does warn that, on occasion, violence is unavoidable. The cry from Latin America is becoming more insistent year after year. For example, 75 percent of the people in Brazil live in poverty and 45 percent sleep with chronic hunger.[86]

Boff stresses that it is imperative that we study the dynamics of poverty and organize serious efforts toward its elimination. The church must make a preferential option for the poor and align our practice with our theological priorities. Boff emphasizes that there has been little grassroots consultation on such matters and that we have neglected a number of critical issues. He points out, for example, that discrimination against women in the church has been shameful and represents a gross violation of human rights. They have been excluded from almost every leadership function and from all meaningful ministerial duties in the church. He also declares that the practices employed by the Doctrine of the Faith Office in the airing of doctrinal disputes are not much different from those used years ago by the Inquisition. One is not able to face his or her accusers, nor does the accused have the right to select an attorney. Often the lawyer for the prosecution and the judge seem to be on the same side. The systems used in similar civil actions in many countries are frequently more sensitive to human rights. The church must lead rather than follow advances in the protection of the rights of the accused. Boff asks whether or not the church as institution can truly be a liberating agent for the poor and the oppressed in our world.

Historically, the reaction of the church to recent social upheavals has been to further centralize its power.[87] Particularly since the mid-nineteenth century, the Catholic Church has appeared as one enormous diocese governed by the pope. The local churches have come to be viewed as branch offices of the central Vatican administration. In spite of occasional declarations indicating that things will change, the centralizing tendency continues unabated. Although the Vatican apparently senses that more authority should be handed down to the local and regional churches, the adaptation of the principle of subsidiarity to the church has been very slow in coming. Until those who have power in the church act more like servants, as Jesus did, the church will never be a symbol of liberation. Boff notes that a new church animated by base communities is being born in Latin America and in other places around the world: "[T]he Roman, Catholic, and apostolic Church is the Church of Christ on the one hand, and on the other, it is not. It is the Church of Christ inasmuch as through it the Church of Christ is present in the world. But at the same time it cannot claim an exclusive identity with the Church of Christ because the Church may also be present in other Christian churches."[88]

The New Testament and its various confessions of faith do not establish the unity of the church. However, within the variety of New Testament ecclesiologies, there is an expression of a common desire to reveal Jesus as the liberator and saving agent of all people. After the Reformation, Catholicism became, in Boff's judgment, a reactionary and repressive ideology.[89] In the small hierarchical class, anything new was under suspicion. Pius IX's *Syllabus of Errors* of 1864 is a dramatic example of this. It is important for the Catholic Church to be ever willing to assimilate diverse cultures and systems of thought in its articulation of faith so that the Christian message represents a blend of God's will and human response. The catholic dimension of church has been defined as the power to be incarnated in the most diverse cultures. Christian identity borrows from the cultures and the traditions of all people.[90] What Boff terms doctrinal Christianity is not open to syncretism—"its one-time syncretization is dogmatized and new teachings are not recognized."[91] He adds: "One comes to the conclusion that the future of Christianity depends on its ability to formulate new syncretisms. Its present cultural expression, from Greco-Roman-Germanic culture, belongs to a glorious past. The present seems to indicate that it will be definitively replaced by the new cultures that surround us."[92]

Boff then returns to the problem of the imbalance among nations and peoples in the world, especially in the West.

> The western world is comprised largely of societies organized around unbalanced means of production, organized around the capitalist system which is characterized by the private ownership of the means of production in the hands of a few, by the unequal distribution of opportunities for work, and by the unequal distribution of the products of that labor. This unbalanced system gives rise to class societies, wherein there are relationships of domination and power between the classes as well as conflicts of interest. There is marked inequality in terms of food, clothing, lifestyles, sanitary conditions, employment, leisure, and so on.[93]

The conflict between the dominators and the dominated inevitably affects the church, which has usually identified itself with the ruling classes. However, there is always the possibility that a new message will arise, and for Boff this is precisely what is happening now at the grassroots level in Latin America and elsewhere. Segments of the church are beginning to identify with the lower classes in their struggle against domination.

The base communities in Central and South America are precipitating the liberation process. The majority of the members are poor and physically weak due to the harsh exploitation of their labor. This not infrequently results from arguments over the ownership and possession of the lands from which the oppressed have been expelled. These base ecclesial communities are a valid expression of the members of the church, who consider themselves victims of capitalist greed. They are in harmony with the church of the Acts of the Apostles and the church of the martyrs.[94] These base communities call out to the bishops and the clergy, insisting on a new style of ministry that is more responsive to their needs. Boff contends that capitalism is truly an impediment to the universality of the church to the extent that it only works for the good of a single class. He recommends that a democratic and socialist society would offer more assistance to greater numbers of people.[95]

These base ecclesial communities consist of small groups of people—fifteen to twenty families—who gather once or twice a week to listen to the Word of God, share their problems, and attempt to solve them in light of the gospel. There are in Boff's estimate, over seventy thousand such communities in Latin America that deal with problems like water, paved streets, schools, and hospital facilities.[96] In this new way of expressing their faith, all people have a chance to speak. Although there are coordinators responsible for setting up the meetings and directing the discussions, all members are equal and share common tasks, for example, visiting the sick, teaching, and confronting their economic problems. If they experience exploitation, they label it as such. In certain instances, they threaten the established social order; on occasion, they experience repression.

Boff insists that bishops and theologians must listen to the voices of these base communities. Occasionally they have a priest in their midst, but often they do not. When he is a part of the group, the priest becomes one of them. These popular expressions of church give the members a chance to express themselves and to grow. There is no doubt that these novel expressions of church vitalize and decentralize the larger bodies of the faithful. Although their activities may lead to persecution in some cases, this liberating praxis is essential. "In Latin America, when a member of a base ecclesial community is imprisoned (as happens often) the others care for the prisoner's family, seek legal assistance, and support and encourage the prisoner through visits and various other means as was done in the early church."[97] Acting thus against the forces of oppression creates, in Boff's estimate, a spirituality of martyrdom.

Several years before the publication of his *Church: Charism and Power*, Leonardo Boff addressed specifically the subject of the base ecclesial communities, identifying them as a new experience of church. "Although the great majority of basic church communities owe their origin to a priest or a member of a religious order, they nevertheless basically constitute a lay movement."[98] Since the Medellin Conference in 1968, this new ecclesial reality has become a veritable ferment of renewal for the church in Latin America. These base communities, in Boff's view, have a permanent future, for they will assist the church in the recovery of its prophetic mission. They will not replace the parishes but should remain as small units of no more than twenty to twenty-five families to avoid bureaucratization.

Boff insists, however, that they represent a valid expression of ecclesial community, for they always maintain a direct connection with the ecclesial structure. He adds:

If we are to develop a new ecclesiology, we shall need more than just theological perspicacity and historical-dogmatic erudition. We must face the new experiences of church in our midst. We in Brazil and Latin America are confronted with a new concretization of church, without the presence of consecrated ministers and without the eucharistic celebration. It is not that this absence is not felt, is not painful. It is, rather, that these ministers do not exist in sufficient numbers. This historical situation does not cause the church to disappear, the church abides in the people of God as they continue to come together, convoked by the word and discipleship of Christ. Something *is* new under the sun: a new church of Christ.[99]

These base communities are built upon faith, the prayerful reading of the Word and meditation on its meaning, and mutual assistance of all kinds. This sort of communal experience lies at the very heart of the reality of church. Boff asks what kind of organization Jesus wanted for his church, and he responds that there is a considerable diversity of opinion in this matter. Under the historical church structures, the faithful have little or no voice. "Decision is restricted to the pope-bishop-priest axis."[100]

This new format changes the relationships among bishops, priests, and laypersons, tending toward a new dynamic in the church. In Latin America, it is beginning to develop a more active, prepared, courageous, and alert body of faithful who can participate and even originate popular movements that can work more effectively for the elimination of social evils that are enslaving the poor.

When it comes to identifying the causes of the miseries they suffer, the members of the basic communities see the main one— not the only one, but the main one—as the capitalistic system. But worse than the system itself is its individualistic spirit of accumulation, its social irresponsibility, and its insensitivity toward human beings, who are treated as "manpower" to be sold at auction. The communities denounce this as unjust, as contrary to God's design in history.[101]

Notes

1. Yves Congar, *Divided Christendom: A Catholic Study of the Problem of Reunion* (trans. M. A. Bousfield; London: Geoffrey Bles/The Centenary Press, 1939).

2. Ibid., 28.

3. Ibid., 150.

4. Ibid., 189.

5. Ibid., 246.

6. Yves Congar, *The Mystery of the Church: Studies by Yves Congar* (2d rev. ed.; trans. Geoffrey Chapman, Ltd. and Helicon Press, Inc.; Baltimore, MD: Helicon Press, 1960 and 1969).

7. Ibid., 24.

8. Ibid., 46.

9. Ibid., 66.

10. Ibid., 72.

11. Ibid., 104.

12. Ibid., 119.

13. Ibid., 131.

14. Ibid., 166.

15. Ibid., 185.

16. Yves Congar, *Power and Poverty in the Church* (trans. Jennifer Nicholson; Baltimore, MD: Helicon Press, 1964).

17. Ibid., 43.

18. Ibid.

19. Ibid., 64.

20. Ibid., 66–67. One of those protesting against these secularizations was St. Bernard of Clairvaux, the mentor of Pope Eugene III (1145–53).

21. Ibid., 70.

22. Ibid., 97.

23. Ibid., 127.

24. Yves Congar, *Lay People in the Church* (rev. ed.; trans. Donald Attwater; Westminster, MD: Newman Press, 1967).

25. Ibid., 25.

26. *Papal Encyclicals* (vol. 3, 1903–37; ed. Claudia Carlen Ihm; Ann Arbor, MI: Pierian Press, 1990), 47–48.

27. Congar, *Lay People in the Church* 362.

28. Hans Küng, *Structures of the Church* (rev. ed.; trans. Salvator Attansio; New York: Crossroad, 1982), 82.

29. Ibid., 86.

30. Ibid., 202.

31. Ibid., 216.

32. Ibid., 215.

33. William La Due, *The Chair of Saint Peter* (Maryknoll, NY: Orbis, 1999), 297.

34. Ibid., 162.

35. Ibid.

36. Küng, *Structures of the Church*, 251.

37. Hans Küng, *The Church* (trans. Ray and Rosaleen Okenden; New York: Sheed & Ward, 1967).

38. Ibid., 125.

39. Ibid., 187.

40. Ibid., 286.

41. Ibid., 307.

42. Ibid., 330.

43. Ibid., 357.

44. Ibid., 397.

45. Ibid., 405.

46. Ibid., 413.

47. Ibid., 440.

48. Ibid., 448.

49. Hans Küng, *Christianity: Essence, History, and Future* (trans. John Bowden; New York: Continuum, 1995).

50. Ibid., 78.

51. Ibid., 96.

52. Ibid., 153.

53. Ibid., 252.

54. Ibid., 271.

55. Ibid., 504.

56. Ibid., 510.

57. Hans Küng, *Infallible? An Inquiry* (trans. Edward Quinn; New York: Doubleday, 1971). An expanded version of Küng's position is entitled *Infallible? An Unresolved Inquiry* (trans. Edward Quinn; New York: Continuum, 1994.)

58. Küng, *Infallible? An Unresolved Inquiry*, 48–49.

59. Ibid., 144.

60. Ibid., 150.

61. David Tracy, *The Analogical Imagination* (New York: Crossroad, 1986), 184 n. 27.

62. Karl Rahner, *Faith in a Wintry Season* (ed. Paul Imhof and Hubert Biallowons; trans. Harvey D. Egan; New York: Crossroad, 1991), 39.

63. Karl Rahner, *Foundations of Christian Faith* (trans. William V. Dych; New York: Crossroad, 1986), 322.

64. Ibid., 327.

65. Ibid., 331.

66. Ibid., 340.

67. Ibid., 349.

68. Ibid., 353.

69. Ibid., 358.

70. Ibid., 373.

71. Ibid., 382.

72. Ibid., 385.

73. Karl Rahner, *The Shape of the Church to Come* (trans. Edward Quinn; London: SPCK, 1974).

74. Ibid., 50.

75. Ibid., 52.

76. Ibid., 57.

77. Ibid., 80.

78. Ibid., 82.

79. Ibid., 95, 114.

80. Ibid., 95.

81. Ibid., 98.

82. Ibid., 104–5.

83. Ibid., 116–17.

84. Leonardo Boff, *The Church: Charism and Power* (trans. John W. Dierksmeier; New York: Crossroad, 1990).

85. Ibid., 16.

86. Ibid., 22.

87. Ibid., 49.

88. Ibid., 75.

89. Ibid., 86.

90. Ibid., 101.

91. Ibid., 105.

92. Ibid., 106.

93. Ibid., 111.

94. Ibid., 120.

95. Ibid., 122.

96. Ibid., 126.

97. Ibid., 137.

98. Leonardo Boff, *Ecclesiogenesis: The Base Communities Reinvent the Church* (trans. Robert R. Barr; Maryknoll, NY: Orbis, 1986), 2. The study was originally published in Portuguese in 1977.

99. Ibid., 13.

100. Ibid., 30.

101. Ibid., 42.

5

THE NEXT GENERATION OF
PROTESTANT ECCLESIOLOGY

John A. T. Robinson (1919–83) and
John Macquarrie (1919–)

During an extended period of convalescence in 1962, Bishop JOHN A. T.
ROBINSON of Woolwich wrote an extremely popular and highly contro-
versial little essay, *Honest to God*.[1] His views on the church were never formally set out in detail, but he deals indirectly with the subject in a number
of his studies. In *Honest to God*, he notes that the theologians who were
most important to him in clarifying his position were Dietrich Bonhoeffer,
Paul Tillich, and Rudolf Bultmann. Robinson first attempts to reinterpret
the meaning of God and chooses Tillich's approach, centering on God as
the Ground of all being. The divinity is not above us or out beyond us but
lives in the very depths of things. Tillich describes prayer as an openness
to the Ground of our being. Robinson also favors the description of
Bonhoeffer, who was fond of naming Jesus "the Man for others."

For the Anglican bishop, Jesus is the window into God, who is at work
in the world. He insists that Jesus never claims to be God personally, yet
he always claims to bring God completely.[2] Robinson compares our current situation to that of Paul in the Areopagus, when he attempted to
describe for the Athenians the unknown God whom they had traditionally revered (Acts 17:16–32). We find ourselves in a similar position today,
for unbelief is on the rise. What we require today is "a radically new mold
of Christian belief and practice."[3]

We must abandon our dependence on what Tillich termed "the super
world of divine objects." A new language is called for that will be more
intelligible and credible to modern man. It is critical that the church reor-
ganize itself far more effectively to be the servant of the world. Robinson
agrees with Bonhoeffer, who was convinced that within a generation the
form and fabric of the church will have changed beyond recognition.[4]
That transformation, in Robinson's view, must consist in "belonging
wholly to the world," although he never seems to spell out exactly what he

means. He does attest that the organization of the church must become increasingly lay.[5] This would not involve getting rid of sacramental ministers, but there must be a stripping down of formalities and a much greater emphasis on the role of the laity in the world. With regard to the mission of the Church of England, Robinson declares:

> Anything that helps to keep its frontiers open to the world as the Church of the nation should be strengthened and reformed: anything that turns it upon itself as a religious organization or episcopalian sect I suspect and deplore. For the true radical is not the man who wants to root out the tares from the wheat so as to make the Church perfect: it is only too easy on these lines to reform the Church into a walled garden. The true radical is the man who continually subjects the Church to the judgement of the Kingdom, to the claims of God in the increasingly non-religious world which the Church exists to serve.[6]

The primary function of the church is not to make people religious, but rather to prepare them to enter fully into the secular world and to be at home there in confronting the challenges of each day in a more and more religionless society. It was not Robinson's intent in this book to describe a new model of church. Rather, we must be open to new approaches that will involve Christians more deeply and more effectively in the Christianization of the world. In spite of its lack of clear plans and programs, his little book had a profound effect upon English-speaking Christians.

Earlier, in 1960, Robinson had published *On Being the Church in the World* during the year after his ordination as bishop. He writes in it that the priesthood of the church is nothing else than the priesthood of Christ exercised through its members.[7] The function of the church is to offer spiritual sacrifices (1 Pet 2:5) and to declare the wondrous deeds of him who has called us out of darkness into his marvelous light (1Pet 2:9). In the New Testament, all the people of God are called to the priesthood, while the church is the privileged community wherein forgiveness is offered.

In the Church of England, the congregation of the faithful is identified as the local congregation, whereas the universal church is viewed as a federation of these local units. Robinson speaks of the house church, as seen in 1 Corinthians 16:19 and Colossians 4:15, as the smallest cell of the church, which should be a microcosm of the life and activity of the entire church. He notes that the house church achieves all the marks of catholicity— the teaching, the fellowship, the breaking of the bread, and the prayers. Until the third or fourth century, the celebration of the Eucharist most probably took place in private homes. In Robinson's judgment, "at every

Eucharist, at whatever level, the whole Church is celebrating; and hence the stipulation that the president must be a priest, ordained and authorized as he is by the bishop to act in the name of the universal Church of God."[8] However, he suggests that because of the mounting scarcity of ordained priests, there may well be a need for a supplemental ministry of some sort in the future.

Robinson discusses the possibility of intercommunion with the Methodists and the Presbyterians. He advocates the development of a single ministry that will be accepted by Anglicans, Methodists, and Presbyterians. Such a change might require the acceptance of some form of episcopate on the part of all three churches.

In 1965, Robinson's study *The New Reformation?* was published, and church polity emerges once again as a principal concern.[9] He emphasizes that there has been an exaggerated insistence on the retention of timeworn formulae, and yet he does not have any intention of advocating a revision of the Thirty-Nine Articles of the Church of England. While the sixteenth-century Reformation was concerned with distinguishing itself in terms of separate and distinct Christian bodies, we must discover a different model that is more open to all Christian believers in the world. Robinson prefers the distinction between the manifest and the latent church employed by Paul Tillich: "The latent church is an indefinite historical group which within paganism, Judaism or humanism actualizes the New Being, while the manifest church is a definite historical group in which the New Being is actualized directly and manifestly."[10] What, asks Robinson, is the role of the manifest church or organized church in what he calls the New Reformation? He responds that its normal form of existence is not to be gathered in one place, "but to be embedded as seeds of light within the dark world."[11] The function of the manifest church is to make it possible for people to be encountered by Christ precisely where they are. Robinson asks whether or not a truly contemporary person can be an authentic Christian. He replies that it cannot happen if this requires that one's faith be tied to the traditional formulae that have become less meaningful in our secularized society.

In the new church, Robinson feels that the broad line between the laity and the clergy should be narrowed considerably and perhaps even abolished if the church is to be opened up for its expanded ministry to the world. He questions whether the priesthood should continue as a salaried position. Perhaps the time has come when people with some kind of trade or profession should be ordained.[12] Further, the church must be prepared to admit women into the ministry. Theological training for the candidates for ministry must be transformed into a theology that meets the needs of the laity and presented in institutions other than seminaries, which have been prominent in the education for the ministry since the mid-1800s. He suggests such training facilities as lay institutes and ecumenical centers. In Robinson's view, the organizational structure must take the shape of the world. It must function as a leaven in the world rather than as a facility alongside the structures of the world.

It is the task of this generation of believers to live in the overlap between two ages. This is a time when there will be no common consensus as to what the church should be teaching. For many ecclesiastics, the temptation will be to live in only one world, to stay with the traditional formulae and attempt to refine and update them. This approach in our time will not work. Robinson quotes the theologian Albert van den Heuvel: "A church which thinks that it can go on dictating truths rather than sitting with the people and working out the real questions is certainly not living in solidarity with men today."[13] Furthermore, there is a pressing need for a profound liturgical renewal, because the traditional forms and rituals no longer speak clearly and forcefully to the modern age.

Robinson then turns his attention to the organization of the church, which is no longer directly related to the vital centers of the lives of Christians: "Well over 90 per cent of the clergymen of the Church of England are in the parish ministry (and the figure would be higher for the Methodists and most other denominations). Moreover, in terms of real estate and finance the Church's capital commitment to this particular form of organization is overwhelming."[14] The existing structures of the church must not simply be given a facelift, but are to be transformed and transfigured according to "the shapes of worldly need." The present denominations—and this is true of Anglicans and Methodists as well—have almost all their resources and manpower in the parish ministry, and this congregational situation is quite unrelated to where people actually live today.

The missions of the church that are focused on communities of need are often understaffed and underfunded. "The organization Church has an immense built-in inertia and I am sure it is utterly unrealistic to think that one can by-pass the tedious, time-consuming process of reshaping it."[15] Robinson asks whether the church can support what he calls exploratory ministries and at the same time sustain the traditional activities of the institution. Perhaps we need missionary bishops who would have one foot in the organization and the other outside. Can we support and even encourage both the new and the conventional ones "without breaking in the middle"?[16] The answer is that we must be willing to experiment with a variety of options to discover what will be effective in bringing the Christian message and the grace of Christ into the pockets of greatest need in our world.

Robinson warns that baptisms could well be reduced by 50 percent in a generation or two and that the current system of compulsory education in the schools is not likely to survive for long. If we do not radically regroup and reshape the church's presence in England, we will simply carry on as we are until the current structures fade away. "The basis of the parish system is that there is a building and a priest within walking distance of every Englishman. . . . Moreover, by attempting to cover the waterfront and keep a service station going everywhere, singularly few signs are *in fact* being shown to convince those outside the religious circle that the Church has a relevance or a future."[17]

Bishop Robinson insists that we shall not succeed by pouring almost all of our resources into our traditional network of residential parishes. And he asks, "Is the Church *free* enough to be there, to let itself 'take shape around his [Christ's] servant presence in the world'?"[18] He advocates that while we do our best to streamline and support our parish organizations, we must look to new forms of ministry so that the church can move ever closer to the crisis points of life.

After completing his graduate studies at the University of Glasgow, JOHN MACQUARRIE taught at his alma mater from 1953 to 1962. In 1962, he was appointed professor of systematic theology at Union Theological Seminary in New York, where he remained until 1970, when he was appointed to the prestigious post of Lady Margaret Professor of Divinity at Oxford. He taught at Oxford until his retirement in 1986.

Macquarrie situates his treatment of ecclesiology under applied theology in his work *Principles of Christian Theology*, published in 1966 with a second edition appearing in 1977.[19] He notes that there has been more written in the field of ecclesiology recently than on almost any other theological subject. Although he was unwilling to declare himself on the question as to whether Jesus personally founded the church, he declares that from the earliest days there has always been a community of faith surrounding the memory of Jesus. The Christian church never identified itself as a national entity and preferred to see itself rather as a supranational people of God. "The Church is to be understood as the community in which this raising of mankind to Godmanhood, which we see in the Christ, continues. The Church therefore is rightly called the 'Body of Christ', which is its most distinctive title."[20]

The new creation proclaimed by Paul occurs in the church as Christ's body. Macquarrie speaks of the church as the consummation of the Incarnation. However, the church has not remained free from sin. He further notes, "if we accept the Christian hope and believe that the tendencies toward fullness of being will prove stronger than the tendencies toward dissolution, we may acknowledge that the Church has its own indefectibility. 'The powers of death shall not prevail against it'" (Matt 16:18).[21] The authority of the church—which Macquarrie describes as "in process"—is not absolute but must be coordinated with the authority of sacred Scripture and reason. The aim of the church is eventually to surrender itself into the final kingdom of God.

The Virgin Mary is given a prominent place in Macquarrie's ecclesiology because he feels that she makes an important contribution to the understanding of the church. He likes to refer to her as the "Mother of the Church" and sees her as a prototype of the church: "What we see in Mary, we ought to see in the Church. Her free cooperative obedience in the incarnation is demanded also of the Church, if God is to be present and active in our world today. The Church too, as St. Paul says, is a mother [Gal 4:26]. Yet the fact that the Church is also set forth as a bride reminds us again that such images and analogies are not to be pushed too far."[22]

The image of Mary standing at the foot of the cross is seen as a reflection of the church's life. Macquarrie does not discuss the Assumption and the Immaculate Conception extensively, but he does affirm that "these two dogmas, when purged of mythological elements, can be interpreted as implications of more central Church teaching, . . . as pointing to moments in the life of the community of faith."[23] While the Immaculate Conception recalls the original state of innocence never completely eliminated by original sin, the Assumption anticipates the final consummation of the church. The place of Mary in the thinking of a number of Protestant communions has become more positive in recent years. Furthermore, the cult of the saints as the standards of self-giving love has been given more attention currently by a number of Protestants.

Macquarrie places considerable emphasis on the traditional notes of the church—unity, holiness, catholicity, and apostolicity. The most significant movement in the twentieth century aiming toward the realization of church unity is ecumenism. He warns that ecumenism carries with it a danger, which is the eradication of genuine differences. The authentic diversity of the churches has to be carefully dealt with as a part of our sacred Christian heritage. "A nondescript Church [where all traditional differences are submerged] would probably turn out to be weaker than a group of churches expressing the Christian faith in its authentic diversity."[24] The Bible is the most valuable source of the unity of the churches. Although some communions do not even have sacraments, for example, the Quakers, they possess the Bible as their common treasure. Macquarrie warns, however, that concentration on the Bible is not sufficient, for the distinctive traditions of the churches cannot be ignored.

The mark of holiness does not imply isolation from the world, but rather an abiding responsiveness to the needs and the possibilities of one's particular life situation. Macquarrie speaks of the sacraments as the growing points that sanctify the significant and privileged moments of human life, but he warns against an overemphasis on the sacramental forms, which can become too mechanical and almost devoid of inner meaning. Catholicity connotes universality as well as authenticity of belief and practice.[25]

For Macquarrie, catholicity is embedded in the ancient creeds, especially the Apostles' Creed and the Creed of Nicaea and Chalcedon. He advises that although the creeds delineate errors in belief, they do leave a good deal of room for theological development. The note of apostolicity is not totally distinct as a concept from catholicity. The church carries on the teaching and the practice of the apostles from age to age in an unbroken continuity. According to Macquarrie, the episcopate is the very embodiment of apostolicity. The canon, the creeds, and the episcopate are the primary guardians of the Christian heritage. These four notes or essential characteristics of the church will become more discernible as the believing community approaches its ultimate transformation. Along with the sacred Scriptures, the critical treasures of the church are the sacraments, the creeds, and the episcopate, which constitute the normative shape of the church and make up its fourfold foundation.

Macquarrie then addresses the role of the papacy. Do any of the special properties that Peter may have had transfer to his successors in the see of Rome? There is little doubt that the papal office was important for the organization of the church in the early centuries, but has too much power accrued to the office during and since the High Middle Ages? The successors of the apostles no doubt constituted a college with a responsibility for leading the churches. Although Macquarrie does not accept the notion of infallibility, the church does possess a certain indefectibility that is revealed in the councils rather than through the papal office.

> Whereas indefectibility is a deduction from the doctrine of the last things and teaches that in the end the church will come to that consummation which God has destined for it, what we are talking about here is the belief that on its way to the end the Church may on particular occasions seek so to open its mind to the divine Spirit that it is led into truth. This is surely an implicate of the doctrine of the Church and is the kernel of truth in the idea of infallibility. But again let it be said that this particular term is a misleading one.[26]

Macquarrie maintains that the optimal governing body for the church would be a worldwide college of bishops, rather than a supreme Roman pontiff. "We can think of it [the papacy] as included within the structure of the episcopate, and as having within the episcopate a primacy which many persons outside of the Roman communion would be willing to acknowledge."[27] The papal role could be refashioned in such a way that the Roman pontiff would be constituted as a first among equals, and not as a supreme sovereign. In this context, he could more easily become the accepted leader of the whole Christian church. The papal office would then be seen not as an additional authority over the church, but rather as a function within the worldwide college of bishops.

John Macquarrie sees the authority of the church as limited by the authority of the Bible. After having settled on the New Testament canon, the church felt the need to be subject to the New Testament as its founding charter. Consensus is generally required in the exercise of significant ecclesial authority on the part of the bishops, who must in turn always be sensitive to the faith of the people. The role of the theologian is that of a responsible spokesperson for the believing community.

The church's role was described by Paul as a ministry of reconciliation (2 Cor 5:18), with Christ's reconciling spirit as the controlling agent. Macquarrie does not advocate a sharp division between the clergy and the laity, as has been the case in many churches. In our age there are numerous functions that the laity are better equipped to perform than the clergy because of their expertise, for example, in the sciences and in business. Macquarrie then describes the distinctive roles of the deacons, the priests, and the bishops. He further observes that when the church is in need of special vocations because of the weakness or waywardness of institutional leadership, for example, at the time of the Reformation, the Spirit provides new direction or fresh inspiration. "Only in very grave circumstances should anyone take upon himself the responsibility of rejecting the established forms; and even in such cases, when one considers the schisms that have in the past weakened the Church, it is a question whether such persons would not have done better to exercise patience."[28]

Macquarrie urges that all adopt a more open stance toward other faiths, Christian and non-Christian. He asks whether it is necessary for all humankind to be gathered into the Christian churches before the arrival of the kingdom of God, and his view is that the church shall remain a representative community but need not embrace all members of the human race. He does not believe, however, that there should ever be an end to the Christian mission of loving service in the world: "There can never be an end to the Christian mission that goes forth in loving service, so long as the kingdom is still unrealized. But perhaps in the modern world the time has come for an end to the kind of mission that proselytizes, especially from sister faiths which though under different symbols, are responding to the same God and realizing the same quality of life."[29] He continues:

> I do not think that the Christian missionary should aim at converting adherents of the so-called "higher" religions in which, as I believe, God's saving grace is already recognizably at work. . . . Would Martin Buber, for instance, have been any better or any nearer to God if he had become a Christian? . . . I think it better that this man should have realized God's grace and brought us God's message (as I believe he did) within the context of his own culture and religion. There he was authentic.[30]

In a more recent collection of essays, Macquarrie shares his thoughts on the Anglican tradition and admits that few Anglican theologians have engaged in systematic theology. After discussing a number of the more prominent theologians since the Reformation, he speculates: "Already in Cranmer [Thomas Cranmer, 1489–1556] we have a clear statement of the essential characteristics of Anglican theology, which bases itself first on the Scriptures, next on the teachings of the early church and its doctors, and finally on reason and experience."[31]

Wolfhart Pannenberg (1928–)

A professor emeritus of systematic theology at the University of Munich, Wolfhart Pannenberg's three-volume work, *Systematic Theology*, has been described by David Tracy as *the* major work in the field in the last twenty years.[32] After completing his studies at Berlin, Göttingen, Basel, and Heidelberg, and after spending a few years as an instructor in theology, Pannenberg was appointed professor of systematic theology at the University of Munich, where he has remained to the present.

Pannenberg points out that the treatment of the church did not constitute a separate theological tract until the fifteenth century.[33] The early Latin Fathers had no systematically developed ecclesiology, while the Greeks, even into the eighth century, proceeded after their discussion of Christology to deal directly with the question of baptism and its effects. It was not until the fifteenth century, after the Council of Constance (1414–18), that separate expositions on ecclesiology began to appear. The Reformers, for example, Philip Melanchthon, were among the first to introduce the subject into dogmatics. John Calvin's last edition of *The Institutes* (1559) gave a certain prominence to ecclesiology, explaining the various church offices and outlining the qualifications for them.

Pannenberg holds that the presentation of the church should precede the discussion of baptism, the Lord's Supper, and the salvation of individuals. Although we can deduce the existence of the church from the outpouring of the Holy Spirit at Pentecost (Acts 2:1–42), Pannenberg feels that it is not possible to attribute the founding of the church directly to Jesus. The calling of the twelve apostles was a symbolic action on the part of Christ that pointed to the final restoration of Israel. Because the official representatives of the Jewish people rejected Jesus, the separation of the disciples of Jesus from the Jews was inevitable.

In spite of the fact that the church is essentially an eschatological community, it must always be distinguished from the kingdom of God, which Pannenberg describes as the future and final fulfillment of humanity under God's rule.[34] The liturgical life of the church can be considered the privileged agent for the mediation of salvation within the community of believers. As reflected in Hebrews 3:7–4:11, the church has always seen itself as the pilgrim people of God, advancing through the wilderness like the Hebrews under Moses, marching resolutely toward the achievement of "God's rest." Although Augustine did attempt to distinguish the future shape of the kingdom from the present form of the church in his masterpiece *The City of God*, later theologians like Schleiermacher were tempted to equate the church with the kingdom.[35] For Hans Küng and Karl Rahner, there should not be an identification between church and kingdom. In Pannenberg's judgment as well, the church is not to be identified with the kingdom, but it is rather a sign or symbol of the realization of the kingdom.

Vatican II's observation that the church is a sacrament of salvation has been frequently contested by Protestant scholars who insist that Christ is the sacrament of unity and the one authentic sacrament, "because it [Vatican II] looks at the church in isolation, not in terms of its participation in Jesus Christ."[36] Jesus is the quintessential embodiment of the gift of salvation, and the church is intimately involved in the working out of this mystery. Pannenberg has difficulty with the position of Leonardo Boff, who affirms that the church's mission is first and foremost to transform the world into the kingdom of God. In Pannenberg's view, however, the kingdom is achieved by God alone. He states, "actualization of the fulfillment of the destiny of humanity in the sacramental life of the church is only in the form of a sign, a sign centered in the Eucharistic celebration of the Lord's Supper."[37]

Pannenberg then concentrates on the inner structure of the church and stresses that Jesus' proclamation of the kingdom did not carry with it any sort of political mission of liberation. The church is the messianic community of God, sent into the world for the salvation of mankind.

Basic to the Reformation concept of the church is the notion that the ecclesial body is a gathering together of believers, an assembly of saints. Paul was fond of addressing the members of the early church as saints (Rom 1:7; 2 Cor 1:1) who are separated from the world for fellowship with the Lord (Phil 1:1). As Pannenberg sees it, "Protestantism makes the relation of individuals to the church dependent on their relation to Christ, while Roman Catholicism conversely makes the relation of individuals to Christ dependent on their relation to the church."[38]

For Pannenberg, the Eucharist is the essential link between the fellowship of believers and the Lord. In each liturgical celebration, Christ is present and the whole fellowship of Christians reveals itself. The church is indeed a *communio*, made up of a network of local churches. It is not first and foremost a worldwide institution with an overarching central leadership.

> The reality of the church is manifested in local communities that are gathered around the Word and sacrament and that also form a fellowship among themselves. But since the formation of a supracongregational leadership with duties of visitation mediates this basic structure to the church, nothing more seems to have been done ecclesiologically at the time of the Reformation. The Lutheran churches, however, did at least recognize the need for an episcopal office of visitation, whereas the Reformed inclined more to synodical forms of supracongregational leadership.[39]

Although the church is primarily visible in the local community and in its eucharistic worship, the unity of the church is also expressed in regional and supraregional ministries that serve the local churches. Pannenberg attests that we can also envision the possibility of a ministry that represents the global fellowship of all Christians. "The Roman Catholic Church claims to have such a ministry in the primacy of the bishop of Rome, although as yet this has not been developed and recast in a form that is acceptable to all, including the churches that are separated from Rome."[40]

The celebration of the Eucharist focuses on the local assembly as the true center of the actualization of the church. This local expression represents the authentic manifestation of the one church of Christ. Pannenberg prefers to call the individual worshipping community the true local church, rather than the diocese. The confession of belief on the part of individuals and communities represents for Protestants an indispensable element in the life of Christians. "If we confess with our lips that Jesus is Lord and believe that God raised him from the dead, we shall be saved" (Rom 10:9). It is the Creed of Nicaea and Constantinople I (381) that sets out the universal Christian faith, and this confession has been acknowledged throughout the centuries. It stands as an authentic expression of the Christian's confession of Christ and Christ's relation to the Father and the Spirit.[41] Pannenberg insists that there must be a standard or model for the celebration of the liturgy. There should also be a determination as to who is to lead the liturgy and who is to be responsible for pastoral care and catechesis. These issues are to be largely settled at the regional level for the sake of uniformity.

A typical situation today is the alienation of large numbers of Christians from the organized churches, "occasioned by the scandal of the division of Christianity into denominations that denounce each other."[42] Further, there is a growing tendency to treat religious confession as a private affair, so that subjectivism has become for many the heart of religion, while affiliation with an organized ecclesial body has come to be considered relatively unimportant. This modern approach to Christianity is seen as validated in the life patterns of Jesus as reflected in the Gospels, because he is frequently portrayed as dealing with individuals and small groups on an informal and casual basis. Nonetheless, Pannenberg affirms that a true relationship with Jesus is to be mediated through the fellowship of a church. However, "the form of individual Christianity that in various degrees and shades is aloof from the church—so long as we do not have the extreme of turning away from the church in principle—is part of the historical reality of Christianity, especially today in the West."[43]

Martin Luther placed great emphasis on the priesthood of all believers (1 Pet 2:9–10). He stressed that each Christian has the right to approach God directly in prayer. These Christians can mutually teach one another about God. Moreover, Luther reserved for all believers the right to judge the preaching of their ordained ministers. Each Christian has immediate access to God, which is fully guaranteed in the New Testament. "We achieve this freedom by participation in the filial relation of Jesus to the Father in faith."[44] The Spirit brings believers into a share of the sonship of Jesus and gives them the gift to address God as our Father (Rom 8:15–16). The Holy Spirit draws Christians together into the fellowship of Christ's body.

Pannenberg describes in some detail the works of the Holy Spirit that are realized in individual Christians. First, he deals with faith, which for Luther consisted primarily in loyalty to the divine promises. Our faith is grounded in the message of God's revelation. The response of faith involves the acceptance of the lordship of God and the new life it brings. Whereas Hebrews 11:1 offers perhaps the best description of faith as "the assurance of things hoped for and the conviction of things not seen," the virtue of hope is most dramatically reflected in the life of Abraham.

Christian hope, then, is not such as individuals cherish only for themselves. The imparting of hope by faith in Jesus Christ frees us from this imprisonment in self and lifts us above the self. Faith thus gives rise to a hope that is concerned not merely about one's own well-being but is bound up with the cause of God in the world that has the salvation of all as its goal and embraces the believer's I [i.e., ego] only in this broad context.[45]

Christian hope extends after this life and anticipates a life beyond. The love of Christians is a benevolent love that searches out and emphasizes the well-being of others, rather than oneself. "If Christian love is essentially a participation in God's love for the world, then we have to ask whether we can distinguish at all between love of God and love of neighbor. Does not true love consist of sharing in God's love for the world? And in the depth of turning to the cohuman Thou do we not also love God?"[46]

Pannenberg then addresses the nature of the appearance of Christian salvation. Baptism is the event that effects the regeneration or rebirth of the individual, and this new fellowship is certainly enhanced through participation in the Lord's Supper. These two rituals effect what they signify. They are signs of the nearness of God. "Theological tradition has used the term 'sacrament' for the distinctive sign that is so important in the life of believers and the church."[47] Martin Luther insisted on communion under both species, because both bread and wine constitute the form of the Eucharist. Pannenberg observes that the change of the physical elements into the body and blood of Christ has been long debated.

Hence Christ's bread saying denotes the presence of the thing signified in the sign. In the bread, for which only the word "this" stands in the saying, Jesus Christ himself, and with him God's rule, is present, but not in such a way that he comes into the bread as a supernatural substance (impanation), rather in such a way that what is signified is there in the sign as an indication of its presence. . . . Thus what is distributed and received is Christ's body. The sign is filled and consumed by the presence of the thing signified as it is distributed and eaten.[48]

The presence of Christ in the Eucharist lasts through the whole liturgical celebration. Pannenberg does not favor the explanation of Schillebeeckx and others that the change is merely a matter of transignification.[49] This would dilute our faith in the real presence of Christ in the Eucharist. The resurrection is the foundation of our firm belief that Jesus possesses the power to be present to his believers in the form of bread and wine.

Pannenberg then discusses the marks or properties that are traditionally assigned to the church. He affirms that the quality of holiness is the result of the sanctification of the believing body by Christ, and by virtue of this, the church is separated in a sense from all the contentiousness and division of the world.[50] Christ's sending of the apostles to all of humankind is continually repeated in the church, and this gives the sending the dimension of apostolicity. The property of catholicity expresses the fact that whenever a Christian congregation gathers for worship, it proclaims the same gospel and celebrates the same Eucharist. Finally, the church is one to the extent that the same Christian message and sacraments of life are always available to transform the lives of believers. Pannenberg advises that these four properties do not demonstrate unequivocally that a church is the true church. Roman Catholics have emphasized over the years that these four marks point unerringly to the Catholic Church as the true church of Christ. For Protestants, however, the church of Christ is certainly present wherever there exists the true teaching of the gospel and the administration of the sacraments as instituted by Jesus.[51] "Today, however, Roman Catholic theology has come to doubt whether the four attributes are indeed empirically unambiguous realities that are better known than the church itself and that may thus distinguish between the true church and the false."[52]

Pannenberg attests that there is a virtual identity between the ministry of bishops and pastors that goes back to the apostolic age. The Council of Trent opposed the view of the Reformers that the distinction between bishops and presbyters was merely of human law. Vatican II did not take a stand on the question, leaving it open for further study. According to Pannenberg, the churches have to reach some kind of agreement as to the relationship between the episcopate and the presbyterate. Is the episcopate the fullness of the leadership function in the church, or is the presbyterate the highest ministerial rank? In addition, there must be some form of regional ministry, and what is to be said concerning the existence of any ministerial office at the universal level? He asserts:

> We ought freely to admit the fact of the primacy of the Roman Church and its bishop in Christianity. Not the fact itself so much as the way of describing it is the point at issue, along with the question of the implied rights. The Eastern churches have always conceded to the church of Rome and its bishop a primacy of honor among other Christian patriarchs and bishops. But they have rejected the larger claims of the popes as the two Vatican councils have formulated them.[53]

The Anglican Church also has reservations regarding the infallibility of the papacy, as well as the pope's claim to primacy of jurisdiction.

> The other Reformation churches have been much more cautious on the issue. Yet the Lutherans accept in principle a ministry to the unity of the church on the universal level. In this regard, along with the idea of a general council to which the Lutheran Reformation steadfastly adhered, there need not be ruled out the possibility that the Petrine office of the bishop of Rome might be a visible sign of the unity of the whole church to the degree that by theological reinterpretation and practical restructuring the office is subordinated to the primacy of the gospel.[54]

Many Christian churches, especially the Orthodox, agree that the ecumenical councils represent the highest doctrinal authority (Matt 28:18–20). However, the actions and enactments of ecumenical councils must be received by the whole body of believers. This *reception* has been defined by Yves Congar as follows: "By 'reception', I understand the process by means of which a church (body) truly takes over as its own a resolution that did not originate in regard to itself, and acknowledges the measure it promulgates as a rule applicable to its own life."[55] In 1 Corinthians 15:1, Paul declares that the gospel of Jesus has been *received* by members of the church as well as preached to them. When there is a notable lack of agreement regarding a doctrinal decision of an ecumenical council, this means that the decision has not been fully *received*, and the enactment is not irreformable. "If there is no reception in the long run, then unavoidably the claim of the teaching office that in a given statement it was expressing the faith awareness of the whole church is a dubious one."[56] Vatican I, however, taught that the definitions of the Roman pontiff are irreformable in themselves and do not call for the consent of the church.[57]

Pannenberg observes that, given our divided condition, it is not certain whether any utterance of the supreme teaching office can be regarded as infallible. Concerning the claims of jurisdictional primacy on the part of the Roman pontiff, such a prerogative can be questioned. In Pannenberg's judgment, the functions of the papacy should be separated.

> The jurisdiction of the universal Christian ministry of leadership ought essentially to mean that the one who discharges this ministry ought to be the chief advocate of unity in interchurch relations. Today the bishop of Rome should be willing to do, and should actually be doing, much more in this regard than is in fact

the case. This is less a function of power (*potestas*) than of the ability to persuade (*auctoritas*).[58]

Furthermore, in Pannenberg's view, the church's claim of papal power grew out of the special significance of Rome as the capital of the empire and because of the martyrdoms of Peter and Paul in Rome. There was a need for an authoritative voice that would be acknowledged everywhere. "From a Reformation standpoint the authority of such an office, and of those who hold it, can be one only of human law because we cannot trace it back to any express institution by Jesus himself."[59]

Pannenberg then engages in a brief discussion of the notion of the church as the people of God, and he expresses his preference for the title "body of Christ," because for him it is the most profound description of the nature of the church. It is at the Lord's Supper that the church expresses itself and identifies itself as the body of Christ: "On the basis of its liturgical life the church's essential being as the body of Christ thus works itself out in the common life of congregations and their members in the world. It does so among other things by diaconal activities and other signs of the salutary effects of the eschatological salvation that is present in the church in response to the needs of the world."[60] The church, however, has not fared particularly well as a sign reflecting the ultimate transformation and future consummation of humankind. "By its divisions, by the intolerance and power seeking of its clergy, but also by its excessive accommodation to the changing modes of the world on the one side and the narrowness of the hothouse forms of its piety in the other, forms that hardly give evidence of the liberating breath of the Spirit, the church has constantly stood in the way of the commission that is grounded in its nature."[61] There is hope, however, that as the Christian churches come together, they will be more effective in revealing to the world the true nature of the Christian church.

Sixteen years before the publication of volume 3 of his *Systematic Theology*, Pannenberg published a section from his *Ethics and Ecclesiology* under the English title *The Church*.[62] The work was rather ecumenically oriented and focused on bringing the various Christian churches together. He emphasizes that countless denominational quarrels among Christians do serious damage to their causes and to the cause of unity. "Christian theology, despite all its efforts to emphasize the universal truth of the Christian tradition, is tied to denominational Christianity, because to this day no better institutional form for the fellowship of Christians has been found than that provided by the denominational churches."[63]

Pannenberg complains that an examination of the churches reveals lordship by the bishops and church presidents, while members hardly know one another. These churches do not indicate any capability for reconciliation among themselves. The number of Christians outside the churches is growing dramatically. Church officials should examine why it is that these Christians outside the visible church can get along without the organization. The Lord's Supper must be rediscovered as the heart of worship and life. Further, the overcoming of the doctrinal disputes among Christian churches is absolutely necessary if the church is to become a sign of the unity of humankind. The ecumenical movement of the twentieth century grew out of the growing awareness that the divisions among Christians are simply intolerable.[64] All Christian bodies must confess their guilt for precipitating conflicts and rifts, because all are to blame.

The continuing multiplication of Protestant denominations remains for Pannenberg a sign of the failure of the Reformation. However, the validity of the other churches must be recognized to some degree so that dialogue among the confessions can be more effective.[65] The Christian churches are encouraged to look forward to a new universal council, realizing that Christian unity must not be sought primarily based on doctrine, but rather on a common confession of Christ. "The establishment of a separate Protestant Christianity was a makeshift solution, because the original goal of the Reformation was the reform of the entire church."[66] Protestants must work toward a new understanding of the theology of the office of the episcopate and of the Eucharist as the heart and center of Christian worship.

Since 1970, the bilateral conversations among denominations have achieved much agreement in a number of critical concerns. The major area of difference centers around the validity of church offices.[67] The Roman Catholic assertion that the office of priest differs in essence from the priesthood of all believers creates considerable difficulty for Protestants, who feel that the two priesthoods should be more closely related. Also, there is little consensus regarding the meaning of the effects of ordination.

There are some who feel that celebrating the Lord's Supper together would contribute significantly to the promotion of Christian unity. However, Pannenberg and others insist that this is unacceptable, because the sharing of the Eucharist is "the expression and confirmation of full ecclesiastical fellowship, including unity of doctrine as well as mutual recognition of church officers."[68]

Pannenberg affirms:

> It appears that the churches lead a comfortable existence as they are presently constituted and are in no particular hurry to achieve unity. But they must be reminded that without the unity of

Christians, no church is a church in the full sense of the word. None of the present separated churches is today identical with the one church of Christ. Are the Orthodox churches and the Roman Catholic Church correct in regarding the Protestant churches as defective, incomplete realizations of the essence of the church? If, however, they regard Protestant Christians as Christians at all and acknowledge that there is anything of the church in their communities, in however defective a form, do they not have to admit that their own church is also defective as long as it has not achieved the visible unity of all Christians?[69]

Jürgen Moltmann (1926–)

After completing his studies at the University of Göttingen, Moltmann taught at Bonn before his appointment to the University of Tübingen in 1967, where he worked until his retirement as professor emeritus in 1994. He received international acclaim for his *Theology of Hope* in 1964. Moltmann's major study on the church, *The Church in the Power of the Spirit*, was published in German in 1975, and the English edition appeared two years later.[70]

Moltmann, who comes out of the Reformed tradition, affirms that what is necessary today is an inner renewal of the church by the Spirit of Christ, and one of the most indispensable dimensions of that renewal is the restoration of emphasis on the theology of mission. "The more the Christian West disintegrates culturally and geographically, the more the church will find its self-understanding in the context of the whole world."[71] One highly important development consists in the fact that the modern world has freed itself from clerical domination. Although the preaching of the gospel was the primary function of the mission of Christ, his role embraced a whole range of activities aimed at liberating humankind from slavery in all its forms and shapes.

A distinct advantage of our time is that the ecumenical movement has turned the Christian communions from anathemas to dialogue. A critical feature of the present scene is the development of the theology of revolution coming out of Latin America, which has revived the revolutionary themes of the Bible. Working for liberation means taking sides with the oppressed. The church must come to see itself as the instrument of transition into the kingdom of God, rather than as the earthly community of the chosen. Moltmann declares that it is the sacramental events that truly constitute the church—the preaching of the Word, baptism, and the coming of Christ in bread and wine. For him, the church is the community of justified sinners, the fellowship of those liberated by Christ who experience salvation and live in thanksgiving.[72] The church has to understand itself as part of the history of the creative Spirit.

A generation ago, there was much talk about the signs of the times, which recalls the Deuteronomic view of history. Many wonder whether the present theology of the signs of the times refers more to the forthcoming exodus into freedom or points to an impending catastrophe. Today there is something of a revolt against the "North Atlantic centers of power" in favor of an emphasis on the liberation of the people of Africa, Asia, and South America. Moltmann concentrates his attention on the church's current mission and its meaning. The sending of the Son and the Spirit has illuminated not only the salvific plan of God, but also the inner reality of the Trinity. The mission of Jesus is by no means a chance event in history, but it reveals the *mysterion*, the divine plan of God for creation.

Moltmann teaches that although Jesus is the foundation of the Christian religion, he did not establish any church.[73] The Synoptic Gospels portray the coming of Christ and his labors in the light of his messianic mission according to the tradition of 2 Isaiah. His undeniable hallmark is his fellowship with the poor and the disenfranchised. The history of Jesus is to be told as the history of liberation, suggesting the Exodus motif. In the crucifixion, Jesus stands with the despised and becomes in a sense God's messenger to the forsaken. In the light of the Letter to the Hebrews, Christ's sacrifice can be seen as a priestly ministry that gives birth to the priesthood of all believers.[74] For Moltmann, there is no fundamental distinction between the priesthood of all the faithful and the special ministry.

Moreover, the church must never identify itself as a class church, a racial church, a male church, or a national church (Gal 3:27–28). And, if the church is to achieve its objective, it must begin with the liberation of the poor and the downtrodden. Moltmann asks where Christ is present in the church, and he replies that he is present in the sacraments, in the apostolate, in the living fellowship of believers, and in the least of the brothers and sisters. Whenever the true gospel is preached, the Lord's Supper is celebrated, and the fraternal fellowship occurs, there is Christ's presence and there is the church.[75] The Quakers, the Society of Friends, have manifested in an exemplary fashion the importance of friendship among believers. The key to that friendship is the mutually acknowledged equality of partners.

Moltmann affirms that the transition from the Christian synagogue to the church took place among the followers of Stephen, and it was in Galatia that the communities of disciples were probably first identified as churches. The rites of baptism and the Lord's Supper carry the promise of

Christ's special presence. Baptismal grace is available to the baptized daily—emanating from their attitude of repentance. The Reformers retained infant baptism, unlike the Baptists, although the practice does remain an open theological problem, because it can be seen as a hindrance to the true meaning of baptism.[76] The New Testament order begins with faith and then baptism. In infant baptism, the faith of the parents, the godparents, and the church make up for the infant's inability to make a profession of faith. The justification of the baptized and prevenient grace come when a person makes the first act of faith, rather than at the moment of baptism.

The Christian congregation is to sanctify the focal moments of life: baptism at birth, confirmation at puberty, wedding at the beginning of married life, extreme unction before death, and then church burial.[77] Although we know nothing about any baptizing on the part of Jesus and his disciples, Moltmann suggests that the community did not receive the mandate to baptize until after Christ's resurrection. While Karl Barth was not especially pleased with the practice of infant baptism, Moltmann proposes a transition from infant to adult baptism, for he understands that baptism creates nothing without faith. Confirmation classes could then be directed toward baptism, which people may approach when they feel able to confess their faith before the congregation and seek out a con-validation of their calling.[78] This transition from infant baptism to vocational baptism would place emphasis on the individual's call to liberating service to society.

The Lord's Supper is not the place to practice church discipline, and the issue of admittance or non-admittance to the eucharistic meal is something of a bureaucratic task that should not encumber the celebrative experience. We must recall that Jesus ate with tax collectors and sinners. For Moltmann, the Lord's Supper is not to be considered a sacrificial meal. It mediates the power of Christ's passion and redemption from sin through his death. It mediates the Spirit and the power of the resurrection.[79] The suffering Jesus is rendered present through his body and blood. This presence is credible on the basis of his promise alone and not on the grounds of any philosophical or theological reasoning. The common bread and the common cup reveal that all who partake gain a share in the Lord's life. This eucharistic celebration is central to the life of Christians, and all believers must share in this event. Moltmann notes that the celebration of the Lord's Supper is not tied to any special ministry. "An effective church reform [of worship] begins first of all by altering the rituals. But these are so difficult to change that they have caused more than one split in the church."[80] It is important to remember that the Christian worship service involves the making present of the one who is the risen Christ of Calvary.

Moltmann speaks frequently about the messianic way of life, which for him means a special fellowship with Christ in confronting the sufferings of the world.[81] He complains that ecclesiology has often become a form of "hierarchology." According to this paradigm, everything must originate from the top and practically all significant apostolic endeavors must be under the control of the ministry. Christ's church cannot be governed by a hierarchy of ministers who are separated from the believers. Each and every member of the church community possesses the gift of the Spirit and is therefore an office bearer. There can be no divide between the minister and the church people. When the vitality of the charismatic community begins to weaken, the hierarchies and the monarchical episcopate arise and flourish. Then the church people become nameless and passive, resulting in the squelching of the Spirit who yearns to speak and act through all of the baptized. When the New Testament uses the word "priest," it does not refer to any special class within the church. In the Letter to the Hebrews, Jesus is the one high priest (10:10–14). And in 1 Peter, we read that the whole church people constitute the royal priesthood (2:9ff.). The gift of the Spirit creates the universal priesthood, while the various roles or ministries are determined by the community itself. Those who preach and perform liturgical functions are not separated from the people. For Moltmann, they are not office bearers who confront the congregation. "As the messianic congregation the people of God cannot recognize the sovereignty of a priestly caste or a ministerial class."[82] One who is commissioned to perform a particular function can be recalled by the members of the community should they choose to do so. "The monarchical justification of the ministry, which has been usual in the mainstream church since Ignatius of Antioch [d. ca.110] was: one God, one Christ, one bishop, one church. This may have had pragmatical reasons in its favor in its own time, but theologically it is wrong, and ecclesiologically it led to a false development."[83]

The setting up of particular ministries by the congregation fulfills various needs, which may change from time to time. The principal roles are: (1) the proclamation of the gospel, (2) the responsibility for baptism and baptismal instruction and the celebration of the Lord's Supper, (3) the task of leading the community's regular assemblies, and (4) the assignment of the charitable works to be performed. Moltmann enumerates the tasks to be assigned as follows:

> For these the congregation needs preachers, presbyters and deacons. The task of proclamation can be distributed between preacher, teacher, pastor, sick-visitor and missionary. The task of leadership in the community can be distributed between elders

and other leading members. The charge to carry out charitable work in the congregation and in society can be defined according to the situation.[84]

These works can be carried out by both men and women, the married and the unmarried, the theologically trained or untrained. The activities can be distributed on a full-time or part-time basis, and the differentiation among members is to be one merely of function and not of rank.

Moltmann then speaks briefly about the reality of the church above the level of the individual congregation. For him, the church is to be understood as existing fully in the local assembly and in all the congregations together. Each congregation must be in harmony with the various congregations everywhere, and this supraregional unity can possibly be represented through some central office of unity or by means of councils held with some regularity.[85] Apostolic succession is envisioned by Moltmann as the means to preserve and hand on the original proclamation of the apostles as well as the apostolic ministries. This handing on is achieved through the laying on of hands. "But the succession of church baptism, the fellowship of the Lord's Supper and the unbroken proclamation of Christ— 'the same yesterday today and forever'—are signs too in at least equal measure."[86] Even a succession of bishops is no guarantee of the permanent identity of faith nor of faithfulness to the apostolic gospel.

Moltmann claims that the best way to express the new relationship between God and the members within the congregation is to term it a fellowship of friends. He is confident that the reformation of the church will be achieved largely through a rebirth of fellowship among all the members. The Reformation rediscovered the congregational principle and came to prefer the term "congregation" to "church." The nineteenth century witnessed the rise of many huge parishes in Europe and in North America. Such a development created the need for alternative forms of church practice, for in these mega-parishes, hardly anyone knows anybody and the realization of a true Christian congregational life is practically impossible.

Church attendance even to the present has continued to decline and the congregation's chance of Christianizing its neighborhood is minimal at best. The phenomenon of base communities in Central and South America is possibly the most effective prophetic leaven for the renewal of many Christian churches: "Church reforms and church reconstruction will begin at the point where people in congregations of manageable size hear, discuss and profess the gospel; where, at the Lord's table, they become friends and perform their tasks in mutual sympathy and co-operation."[87] There is also danger of too much control in the hands of the regional church organizations, which deprives the individual congregations of their independence and, in many cases, of their capacity for responsible action.

In 1978, Moltmann published *The Open Church*, which is a more popular rendering of his *The Church in the Power of the Spirit* and is intended for study groups. In the final chapter of this more recent book is a superb paragraph that recapitulates much of the theologian's ecclesiology.

> "The church" with its structures, organizations, and powers exists exclusively for the sake of the *congregation*. There is in the church nothing higher than the congregation. All ministries of the church are related to the congregation and are put to the test by the mature congregation. From its side, the congregation is mature to the degree that it no longer experiences itself as being taken care of ecclesiastically and tended to by ordained officials but rather becomes the independent, responsible subject of its own history with God. Only then can Christian freedom be experienced in the congregation, for only then will the congregation be experienced as the free zone of the Spirit of God.[88]

Notes

1. John A. T. Robinson, *Honest to God* (London: SCM, 1963).

2. Ibid., 73.

3. Ibid., 122.

4. Dietrich Bonhoeffer, *Letters and Papers from Prison* (New York: Collier Books, 1972), 300.

5. Robinson, *Honest to God*, 137.

6. Ibid., 139–40.

7. John A. T. Robinson, *On Being the Church in the World* (London: SCM, 1960; Pelican Books, 1969), 91.

8. Ibid., 108.

9. John A. T. Robinson, *The New Reformation?* (Philadelphia: Westminster, 1965).

10. Ibid., 47.

11. Ibid., 48.

12. Ibid., 59.

13. Ibid., 81.

14. Ibid., 89.

15. Ibid., 96.

16. Ibid., 99.

17. Ibid., 103.

18. Ibid., 104.

19. John Macquarrie, *Principles of Christian Theology* (2d ed.; New York: Scribner's, 1977).

20. Ibid., 388.

21. Ibid., 390.

22. Ibid., 395.

23. Ibid., 397.

24. Ibid., 404.

25. Ibid., 407.

26. Ibid., 415,

27. Ibid., 415–16.

28. Ibid., 428.

29. Ibid., 445.

30. Ibid., 446.

31. John Macquarrie, *Theology, Church and Ministry* (New York: Crossroad, 1986), 101.

32. Wolfhart Pannenberg, *Systematic Theology* (3 vols.; trans. Geoffrey W. Bromiley; Grand Rapids, MI: Eerdmans, 1988–98).

33. Pannenberg, *Systematic Theology*, 3:21.

34. Ibid., 31.

35. Ibid., 34.

36. Ibid., 41.

37. Ibid., 52.

38. Ibid., 100.

39. Ibid., 103–4.

40. Ibid., 108.

41. Ibid., 122.

42. Ibid., 125.

43. Ibid.

44. Ibid., 129–30.

45. Ibid., 179.

46. Ibid., 187.

47. Ibid., 238.

48. Ibid., 300.

49. Edward Schillebeeckx, *The Eucharist* (London: Sheed & Ward, 1977), 144–60.

50. Pannenberg, *Systematic Theology*, 3:406.

51. Ibid., 409.

52. Ibid., 410.

53. Ibid., 421.

54. Ibid.

55. Yves Congar, "Reception as an Ecclesiological Reality," *Concilium* 77 (New York: Herder & Herder, 1972), 45.

56. Pannenberg, *Systematic Theology*, 3:428.

57. H. Denzinger and A. Schönmetzer, *Enchiridion Symbolorum* (32nd ed; New York: Herder & Herder, 1963), no. 3074.

58. Pannenberg, *Systematic Theology*, 3:428–29.

59. Ibid., 430.

60. Ibid., 432.

61. Ibid., 433.

62. Wolfhart Pannenberg, *The Church* (trans. Keith Crim; Philadelphia: Westminster, 1983).

63. Ibid., 15.

64. Ibid., 23.

65. Ibid., 33.

66. Ibid., 85.

67. Ibid., 100.

68. Ibid., 117.

69. Ibid., 152.

70. Jürgen Moltmann, *The Church in the Power of the Spirit* (trans. Margaret Kohl; London: SCM, 1977).

71. Ibid., 8.

72. Ibid., 33.

73. Ibid., 70.

74. Ibid., 96.

75. Ibid., 125.

76. Ibid., 232.

77. Ibid., 231.

78. Ibid., 241.

79. Ibid., 252.

80. Ibid., 262–63.

81. Ibid., 288.

82. Ibid., 303.

83. Ibid., 305.

84. Ibid., 307.

85. Ibid., 310.

86. Ibid., 313.

87. Ibid., 335.

88. Jürgen Moltmann, *The Open Church* (trans. M. Douglas Meeks; London: SCM, 1978), 115.

6

OTHER APPROACHES TO CHURCH

Rosemary Radford Ruether (1936–)

After completing her theological studies at the Claremont Graduate School in California, Rosemary Ruether taught for twenty-five years at Garrett Theological Seminary in Evanston, Illinois. In 2002, she accepted an appointment in Feminist Studies at the Pacific School of Religion in Berkeley where she currently teaches. In one of her earliest works, *The Church Against Itself,* Ruether announced that she wanted to strip away the triumphal dimensions of ecclesiology in order to look beyond the myths and focus on the true negatives and positives of the present church.[1] She was convinced that Christian churches generally had been out of touch with the real world for a long time and that this was especially true of Roman Catholicism. These religious bodies must engage with contemporary culture if they wish to be taken more seriously, and their message must be made more intelligible and credible to the world if they desire to be widely heard.

For both Martin Luther and John Calvin, the authority of the Christian message must consist of the Word rightly preached, rather than in the unbroken succession of church offices and structures. For Ruether, "the historical church, as an incarnational reality, ceases to be historical and becomes ahistorical or meta-historical, passing through time, but unaffected by its vicissitudes."[2] She points out that "the disparity between the original message of Jesus and its subversion by the institutional church is the unsolved dilemma of church history."[3] By the second century, the prophetic voices in the church became fainter in the wake of the increasing emphasis on the institutional dimension of ecclesial life. Ruether insists that "the Holy Spirit does not underwrite any finalized historical structures and dogmas, but rather breaks apart and brings to an end such history."[4]

From the late Middle Ages, the church was making its way through history but remaining almost untouched by it. Then, in the post-Tridentine period, the church detached itself from reality and retreated almost completely from the forward movement of society. It disengaged itself from many of the aspects of human life and progress. In Ruether's judgment, the church has almost everywhere been identified with the spirit of reaction rather than with the spirit of progress, although many had hoped that the pontificate of John XXIII (1958–63) would initiate a new era for the Catholic Church.

According to Ruether, the concept of apostolicity arose in the second century to disguise the growing discontinuity emerging between the apostolic and the post-apostolic faith. The second- and third-century church was inclined to project its monarchical episcopate back into the first century, "and this fiction serves to maintain the continuous fiction of the substantial identity of Catholic faith with the faith of the primitive church down to our own times."[5] The growing disaffection among Christians began in the latter Middle Ages and continued through the eighteenth and nineteenth centuries. The Reformation of the sixteenth century attempted to go beyond what Ruether calls Catholic Christianity to apostolic Christianity. She believes that modern theology has not really accepted what she terms the irreversible disconnect between apostolic Christianity and the subsequent Christian tradition: "There can be no literal return to apostolic Christianity except among those apocalyptic and Messianic sects which rise up from time to time on the fringes of main-stream Christianity, only to be annihilated in disbelief or incorporated into established Christianity after their first ecstatic generation has passed."[6]

Contemporary Christians are often unable to identify with the thought patterns of traditional theology. The newer, more existentialist and personalist renderings of Christian thought have begun to initiate a significant rethinking of the basic Christian tenets. "Theology, Christology, ecclesiology, the sacraments—the whole structure of Christian doctrine will have to be rethought, leaving no traditional Catholic formula unturned to the new view."[7] In the third and fourth centuries, we witness the rise of regional and universal church councils, and the transition from the apostolic paradigm to Greek thought patterns that found their way into the presentation of the Christian message. This transition resulted in a change of major proportions in the theology, the catechesis, and the preaching of the early church. In the first centuries, there was no concept of a worldwide organization. Although certain Christian centers, for example, Rome, Antioch, and Ephesus, were models of good apostolic authority, there was no primacy of jurisdiction of one church over the others. There was rather an episcopal confraternity that was expressed and fostered through correspondence, regional synods, and personal contacts.

The universal councils, such as those held at Nicaea (325) and Constantinople I (381), gave expression to the worldwide magisterium of the episcopate, and this pattern of church order remains normative for the Orthodox and the episcopal churches today. With Roman Catholicism, the concept of universal authority residing in the Roman pontiff developed in the fifth century and beyond with popes like Leo I (440–61). These papal claims grew eventually into the doctrine of the supreme power of jurisdiction held by Rome over all the churches of Christendom. For Roman Catholics today, the authentic apostolic teaching is to be found more often than not in the current teaching of the popes, although Vatican II did declare itself open to a more historical understanding of revealed truth.[8] For Ruether, more important than the creeds and the articles of belief is "the living relationship with God which cannot be judged by external criteria. The truth of faith is encounter rather than objective knowledge."[9]

At Vatican II, the Catholic Church declared its intention to take part in ecumenical discussions and stated that Protestant churches possess a certain ecclesial reality. The Orthodox have their apostolic succession and sacramental life, and the Anglicans have their episcopal polity. The Evangelical churches have what Ruether calls their baptismal reality, and even the Spiritualists (e.g., the Quakers), who have abandoned all external rites and ministers, do possess a certain ecclesial reality.[10] The Catholic Church, however, can only comprehend a unity of the churches in terms of the reincorporation of other bodies into the Roman communion. Regarding the historical development of the Christian church, Ruether makes the following observation:

> That a historical church resulted from Jesus' impact on his disciples and their mission is an unquestionable fact of history. That they founded a historical church in the institutional sense understood by traditional Catholicism is something else again. On the contrary, as long as this eschatological understanding of the church lasted—i.e., through apostolic times—no historical church institution was contemplated. This is because the church did not understand itself as a historical institution, but as the beginning of the Kingdom existing at the end of history in the turn of the aeons.[11]

For Paul, the office of the apostle was not transferable, while the offices of prophet and teacher were at the center of the local congregations. In fact, the New Testament itself was the work of the prophets and teachers of the primitive church. After the time of the *Didache* (100–150), the churches began to be less dependent on a pneumatic, charismatic ministry and relied almost exclusively on an official ordained ministry. The functions of the bishops continued to expand, and their role began to resemble that of their civil counterparts more and more. In the letters of Ignatius of Antioch (d. ca. 110), the local bishop emerges as the principle of unity in the local church.

> The institutional structure expels the Spirit because it claims an absolute possession of it. When it understands its origins rightly, then it may find a positive and indeed indispensable relationship to Christ. . . . Briefly stated, the institutional office can put itself back into a positive relationship with the Spirit when it understands that it was *not* instituted by Christ, but was instituted by history.[12]

Ruether affirms that all institutional offices in the church are the products of history and are not divinely ordained. The Christian community from the outset has been most completely expressed in the breaking of the bread. This celebration is not just a ceremony but is the very heart and center of our everyday lives, for it renders present the eschatological reality of the church.[13] As the Hellenistic paradigm grew more and more prevalent, the connection between ecclesiology and eschatology was less evident. The Lord's Supper was no longer a genuine communal meal, but it became a rite or a ritual. For Ruether, the church is to be seen as "the eschatological community of God nourished on the food of the Messianic banquet and, at the same time, the broken, sinful community of men here and now who need not deny any of their imperfection, but rather know their eschatological being precisely as the power to freely confess their sins, for they live in their new being by faith and not by sight."[14]

We have developed in the Roman communion a ministry of quasi-deified persons. The supreme leader becomes infallible and impeccable, and all the other members become his slaves. To disobey him is to disobey God. In the church, all should be ministers as well as receivers.

> The power of forgiveness and communion is a power inherent in the relationship of all Christians to one another as an act of their ecclesial being. Therefore, the power of the keys, the power of forgiveness and communion, is not the charisma of a special group, like prophets and healers, but belongs to all who have themselves been forgiven and restored to communion. . . . The power to baptise, to forgive, and to do eucharist is inherent in the ecclesial existence of every baptised and believing person. That the church for

the sake of institutional order, designates certain members as "normal ministers" of the sacraments does not alter the general character of the charisma.[15]

Dividing the church into active and passive members distorts the reciprocity that dictates that all Christians are to be both givers as well as receivers. The institutionalization of offices, however, is not to be ruled out. It assumes that there will always be officials who will be there in season and out of season to preach the Word and to gather the faithful for Eucharist.

Early in her career, Rosemary Ruether espoused the mission of feminism.[16] The feminists do more than protest; their role is to adopt the new way of living now. "This means that we need to form gathered communities to support us as we set out on our exodus from patriarchy."[17] In the history of the church there has always been a tension between two church models: church as Spirit-filled community and church as historical institution. The earliest instances of Christian ministry were charismatic and tended to include women. For example, the Montanists (second century) included women in their prophetic ministry, but episcopal Christianity expelled the representatives of charismatic Christianity. In spite of its many positive contributions, the rise of monasticism in the fourth century brought with it a misogynist tradition.

In the twelfth century, even the autonomy of women religious in their own convents was restricted by their local bishops and their own higher superiors. New movements like the Waldensians issued a strong demand for alternative ways of Christian living, but their abuses and exaggerations were self-defeating. During the Reformation, the Spiritualist and Anabaptist movements emphasized the conflict between the charismatic and the institutional communities. In the seventeenth century, the Quakers contributed mightily to the development of egalitarian tendencies in Puritanism, which ruled out all distinctions of class and gender. Women had expanded roles in church administration among the Puritans, and this development also took root in eighteenth-century Methodism.

The conflict between charismatic leadership and the institutional churches is evident in the Christian communities in the United States during the eighteenth and nineteenth centuries. Revivalism in the United States, especially in the nineteenth century, brought women into prominence and narrowed the gap between clergy and laity. The Mennonites and the Moravians in America aided in the development of a more egalitarian rapport between men and women. Some even speculated that God could be androgynous.[18] The tensions between the historical institutions and the Spirit-filled communities have traditionally advanced the emancipation of women. In Central and South America, the popularity

126 • The Trinity Guide to the Christian Church

of liberation theology has precipitated the dramatic growth of base communities whose goal is to establish a society free of patrimony and injustice inflicted on the poor. Nicaragua was the first country where this type of social revolution occurred, in spite of the resistance of the Vatican.[19] These base communities have developed in other countries in South and Central America, as well as in Holland, Italy, and the United States. Many of these communities are especially frustrated with male leadership in the church and male-dominated theology.

According to Ruether, it is incorrect to assert that Jesus established an institutional church and authorized in some way the development of a hierarchical government to be perpetuated through the ages. Moreover, "it is unlikely that Jesus intended to found a separate religion outside Judaism, much less an institutional church with a Roman juridical structure."[20] Christ in all likelihood did not establish the order of bishops or the papacy. In fact, it is unlikely that the Twelve would have been able to recognize the Christian community as it evolved over the first couple of centuries. Ruether insists that all forms of church polity and ecclesial organization are of human origin: "The optimal polity is the polity that can be most responsible in transmitting and communicating Christian culture while erecting fewest barriers to the workings of the Spirit. So far, no historical polity has proven to do this infallibly, nor has any polity proven an insurmountable barrier to the workings of the Spirit. Each has its strengths and deficiencies."[21]

It is Ruether's view that schisms have erupted again and again because the existing historical institutions have not been able to adjust to the Spirit-filled communities living in their midst. Feminism, which is probably the most radical reform movement of all, can develop more effectively within the context of the existing churches rather than remaining as independent units. Moreover, great numbers of women were not initially key players in the liberation movement, and therefore they did not have a great deal to do with the definition and framing of this early-twentieth-century prophetic emphasis. Ruether points out that "the servitude of women is never mentioned either as something to be criticized or to be rectified in the light of the Exodus."[22]

The New Testament clearly took to itself the Exodus motif and applied it to many varieties of human servitude. The lesser station of women, however, has only recently been related explicitly to the Exodus narrative. Women played a decisive part in the propagation of Christianity in the early years and functioned in leadership roles as local ministers in several of the primitive churches. For example, in the closing chapter of the Letter to the Romans, Paul mentions a number of women, such as Phoebe, Prisca, Mary, and Persis, outstanding "workers in the Lord" who played indispensable roles in the spread of the gospel and in the organization of the early congregations in Paul's day. In the gnostic gospels, Mary Magdalen is portrayed as a critical figure and a close disciple of Jesus.

Ruether points out that the church as reflected in 1 Timothy is modeled after the patriarchal family. Throughout Christian history, patriarchy and the subordination of women in the church were the norm until the rise of feminism in the last century. Even in the writings of many liberation theologians, it is not clear that the liberation of women is an indispensable part of their agenda.[23] The transformation of the church to a coequal congregation for men and women will not be by any means an easy endeavor. This project, which Ruether calls "Women-Church," is not readily welcomed by the patriarchal church, because it would mean the dismantling of the patriarchal structures of power. American Protestant women have been included in their church ministries for more than a generation, and women enrolled in theological schools and seminary programs have also increased among Roman Catholics.

Ruether opposes the reservation of the celebration of the Eucharist as an exclusively clerical domain. The same applies to the sacrament of reconciliation, which the New Testament describes as the experience of forgiveness that Christians should exercise toward one another (Jas 5:16). The overriding clerical control of church administration at all levels represents a significant and often deadening assertion of power over the church people. Vatican II's effort to collegialize the administration of parishes through parish councils, and even, to some extent, dioceses through diocesan councils, has not been especially effective thus far. For Ruether, the identification of the church with an ecclesiastical superstructure controlled by clerics is anything but ideal. Dismantling clericalism, however, does not do away with authentic leadership based on function and skills. Congregations need liturgical creators, teachers, administrators, spiritual counselors, and community organizers, who should be chosen based on their competence and skills. Moreover, a critical dimension of full liturgical life must include a certain commitment to social praxis focusing on several areas of need in the locality. Rosemary Ruether's theology has brought her into contact with the most important issues of our time, including racism, sexism, and ecofeminism.[24]

John Meyendorff (1926–92) and John Zizioulas (1931–)

After his graduate theological studies at the Orthodox Theological Seminary, St. Sergius in Paris, JOHN MEYENDORFF attended the Sorbonne. From 1959 to the day of his death, he taught at St. Vladimir's Seminary in New York. He was a major contributor to the renewal of interest in

Byzantine culture and the Byzantine church. Most of his work is in historical theology and ecclesiology.

He affirms that there was no systematic treatment of ecclesiology in Greek patristic literature. The sources for the study of the Orthodox Church are the canons of the early ecumenical councils, the legislation of certain particular councils, the writings of the Fathers of the church, and certain documents of imperial legislation beginning with the enactments of Justinian (527–65). During the Byzantine period (324–1453), the patriarch of Constantinople was the de facto leader of the Eastern church, and he ruled with the collaboration of a permanent synod. The christological disputes of the fifth century precipitated the final break between the Byzantines and the other Christian churches of the East—the Syrians, the Egyptians, and the Armenians.[25] The Roman primacy in the West developed in a very different fashion from the evolution of the ecclesial organization in the East.

The *filioque* dispute remains to this day the crucial point of difference between the East and the West. The *a Patre per Filium* formula that prevails in the East is especially attentive to the absolute monarchy of the Father, since the Holy Spirit proceeds from the Father alone and not from the Father and the Son, according to Western theology. The historic schism of 1054 was almost entirely the result of a number of disagreements over ritual practices between Latin settlements in the East and the Orthodox hierarchy. From the year 400 on, the monarchical papacy in Rome had been evolving and asserting its prerogatives in the West, while the Orthodox leaders for centuries were hardly aware of or interested in this emerging institutional development.

The vehicle for settling early disputes between the East and the West, especially those of a doctrinal nature, was the universal council, and the last of these bringing together the two Christian worlds was Nicaea II in the autumn of 787 over the question of the veneration of images. The icons are representations of Christ, his mother, the angels, and the saints—portrayals not to be worshipped, but only venerated. After Nicaea II, there was not as much contact between the Latins and the Orthodox.

Meyendorff describes the Orthodox Church as a rather loose communion of independent or autocephalous churches. The overriding organization in Orthodoxy (involving the sixteen or more patriarchates and their missions in Western Europe, America, and elsewhere) is very different from the monarchical arrangement in the West under the Roman papacy. There is an ecumenical patriarch who is the first among equals and who resides in Constantinople, but each of the patriarchates is independent of the others. The competence of regional councils, which have ultimate authority in a given patriarchate or province regarding the appointment of bishops, was arranged at Nicaea in 325. These provinces originally coincided with the provinces of the Roman Empire in the East and were subdivided into dioceses and then into individual churches or congregations. The great sees of Rome, Constantinople, Antioch, Alexandria, and Jerusalem, which were the major centers of the early church, constituted the five patriarchates. This somewhat informal division of the Christian world dates from at least the sixth century. All four of the Eastern patriarchates are still in existence, while newer patriarchates have been added over time—Georgia, Bulgaria, Serbia, and Russia.[26]

> The pentarchy, or the coordinated rule of the five great patriarchs over all of Christendom, was an organizational structure which had grown up over the centuries. Although it was not formally proposed as an ecclesiological system until the eighth and ninth centuries, the pentarchy was implicit in the conduct of the ecumenical councils of Constantinople I (381), Chalcedon (451), Constantinople II (553), and Constantinople III (680–81).[27]

Meyendorff has made the following observation regarding this organizational arrangement: "This system of 'pentarchy', the governing of the universal church by five rulers, equal in dignity, but related to each other by a strict order of precedence, was a Byzantine vision, enshrined in the legislation of Justinian."[28]

The full integrity of each local Orthodox church is dependent on its communion with all the other Eastern bodies. Although the Orthodox East felt the need for universal leadership, particularly in the fourteenth century under the aegis of the capable Philotheus, the patriarch of Constantinople, this effort was not successful, and institutional regionalism continued to prevail in the East.[29] The ancient rules established in the early councils created an ecclesiastical regionalism in the context of a universal unity of faith. The worldwide Orthodox Church reveals itself as a fairly loose fellowship of independent churches united in faith, the sacraments, and a common canonical tradition.

Especially from the eighteenth and nineteenth centuries, a growing nationalism has effected a transformation of sorts in the regional design of Orthodoxy. As a result, various bodies of Orthodox persuasion have begun to oppose one another on the basis of nationalism, although they may have been part of the same patriarchate. Several nations, therefore, have established their own independent churches. Over the years the patriarchs of Constantinople have opposed this trend, but with little success. The consequence is that the Orthodox have become more deeply divided on national grounds, even within the several patriarchates.

In examining the words addressed to Peter in Matthew 16:18, Meyendorff's assessment is that Peter is declared to be the rock to the extent that he professes the true faith. Indeed, each and every bishop who professes the true faith is the authentic successor of Peter. In the twentieth century, the Orthodox have been rather active in the World Council of Churches, particularly through the efforts of the patriarchs of Constantinople. A theological dilemma surfaced, however, as the result of a statement issued by the World Council in 1954. In this declaration of the assembly at Evanston, the Christian church itself was described as both a sinner and as justified.[30] Although individual members are to be viewed as both sinners and justified, for the Orthodox the church itself is infallible and without stain. The position of the declaration of the World Council implies a negation of the full and real presence of Christ in his church.

The Orthodox do not believe that they can add anything essential to what Orthodoxy already possesses. They can assist in pointing out to the other Christian bodies the true road to Christian unity. However, there are certain basic elements that make up the fullness of the church that, in the opinion of the Orthodox, are lacking in the Protestant communions. For example, the Protestant notion that the fullness of the institutional gifts of the church will be acquired only in the eschatological future is not acceptable to Orthodoxy.[31] The Orthodox Church does not claim to possess any infallible criterion of truth. Nonetheless, this church is considered to be the dwelling place of the Holy Spirit, who remains always the unique judge and promoter of truth.

Regarding the primacy of Peter, John Meyendorff teaches that in the East there are a number of sees closely identified with Peter, notably, Antioch and Jerusalem. For Cyprian of Carthage (d. 258), Peter became the rock on which the church was founded because he articulated the true belief in the divinity of Christ.[32] The see of Peter is actually present in every local church as long as the true faith is proclaimed there. For Meyendorff, the Roman pontiff is the successor of Peter only if he remains true to the faith of Peter.[33] For some Orthodox theologians, the Petrine primacy is not necessarily bound to the church of Rome because no apostle had been appointed bishop of any individual city. Apostles had the same power everywhere they went. The bishops they ordained became the pastors and shepherds in the various cities and countries.

A graduate of the theological school at the University of Athens, JOHN ZIZIOULAS studied patristics at Harvard University and has long been active in the World Council of Churches. He is currently bishop of the Metropolitan District of Pergamon in the Patriarchate of Constantinople. Yves Congar considered him to be one of today's most original theologians. According to Zizioulas, the Orthodox are known for their devotion to tradition and to the ancient Fathers and for the centrality of worship in their theology.

For this theologian, apostolic continuity is to be viewed from the historical and from the eschatological points of view. Historically, from the time of the apostles, the Christian community has been dispatching missionaries to the ends of the earth, while eschatologically, the Eucharist is the anticipation of the convergence of the dispersed faithful from all corners of the world into a single place on the final day. Clement's letter to the Corinthians (95–96) emphasizes the historical approach, and the letters of Ignatius of Antioch (ca. 110) stress the eschatological approach, portraying the last day as the time of a final convocation around the eucharistic table.[34] While Christ provides the historical continuity, the Holy Spirit transposes the final days back into our own history.

Zizioulas makes a great deal of the notion of *epiclesis*, the calling down of the Spirit to witness and bring about the consecration of the elements at the Eucharist. This is the focal juncture of the Christian life. "The epiclesis means ecclesiologically that the church asks to receive from God what she has already received in Christ as if she had not received it at all, i.e. as if history did not count in itself."[35] The convergence of the historical and the eschatological reveals the sacramental nature of the church, which is rendered present most fully in the eucharistic celebration. "This makes the eucharist the moment in which the church realizes that her roots are to be found *simultaneously* in the past and in the future, in history and in the eschata."[36]

Zizioulas points out that the church found it necessary to objectify the Word of God through the creation of the canon of Scripture. The faith transmitted to the faithful must be received over and over again in and through new forms of experience. Also, he understands that the continuity of the church in a given place is not to be traced back to an individual apostle, but rather to the apostolic college as a whole. Furthermore, this continuity is not to be realized just from bishop to bishop, but rather in terms of one bishop and his college of presbyters following upon another.

Zizioulas feels strongly that no episcopal ordination can be celebrated without referring explicitly to the name of the new community or diocese to which the bishop is to be sent. Charismatic ministries—those not coming through ordination—must be related to the structure of the church through the bishop and the presbyters, because the entire ecclesial fabric converges in the bishop. It was Cyprian of Carthage (d. 258) who changed the image of the apostolic college surrounding Christ into the college viewed with Peter as its center. For Cyprian, each and every episcopal throne was to be considered a chair of Peter. Furthermore, the more prestigious sees were never considered to be more apostolic than those less notable, for each was understood to be the chair of Peter, possessing apostolic continuity through him.

All the faithful are to be considered ordained by virtue of their baptism and confirmation. In baptism, the community is separated from the world, while in the eucharistic celebration we are related again to the world and to all humankind. Zizioulas adds, however, that the missionary thrust to the world must be focused first and foremost on the concrete local community where the church is situated. Also, the congregation's missionary activity must express itself in a variety of ministries and not just in one or another specific direction.

Priestly ordination makes the ordained "a relational entity."[37] It transforms the person and confers upon the individual a new life direction, and the ordained person is specifically assigned to a particular place and locality. Moreover, in the ordination of a bishop, the individual is admonished that no local church is truly a church unless it is open to full communion with all the rest of the churches. This openness to communion with the other churches serves as the ground for conciliarity. Although most Orthodox regulations and directives are the result of regional and provincial councils, Zizioulas warns that no conciliar decision ever becomes authoritative unless it is *received* by the community or communities.[38] Thus, a true council acquires its force only a posteriori.

The question of the relationship between episcopally and non-episcopally structured churches is a problem for Zizioulas, because how are they to be identified one with the other if one church congregation has a bishop and the other, for example, a neighboring Protestant congregation, does not? He does agree, however, that every effort must be made by the several congregations of whatever denomination to recognize each other as ecclesial communities, even though they are quite different. Furthermore, each local church should include in its eucharistic assemblies all the Orthodox church members without any distinction of race, nationality, or cultural background. Zizioulas prefers the arrangement involving one bishop celebrating in each place or diocese, even though in certain locations there seem to have been from the beginning a number of household churches operating simultaneously in the larger population centers. He feels that the multiplication of eucharistic assemblies celebrated by several priests in one city or location does some damage to the notion of church. The theoretical design here seems to Zizioulas to take precedence over the convenience of the faithful.

Through the centuries, with the development of the metropolitan and patriarchal systems, the center of gravity in Orthodoxy has shifted somewhat away from the local units to the larger jurisdictions. However, Zizioulas is adamant that neither the metropolitan territory nor the patriarchate qualifies as a local church, which in his view is realized only in the diocese with its local bishop. Regarding the development of the metropolitan and patriarchal territories, such divisions are for Zizioulas not really ecclesial entities, for the true nature of the church ends with the local congregation, although each local church must always be in meaningful contact with the other churches so that true communion can be achieved.

In the last two centuries, the Orthodox came to be governed by their own national synods, which are independent of other Orthodox churches. Each of the national churches has acquired its own archbishop or metropolitan. Zizioulas admonishes that if in a given location there is more than one cultural or ethnic grouping, the church in that location must make every effort to reach these diverse elements through its missionary activity. Each local church attains its full maturity "when the saving event of Christ takes root in a particular situation with all its natural, social, and cultural characteristics."[39]

Zizioulas warns that local assemblies formed solely of a particular culture or ethnic group to the exclusion of others should really not be regarded as Orthodox churches in the full sense. Moreover, the problems and challenges of all the local churches in the region should be the concern of each church. For Zizioulas, ministerial structures that are created above the local churches and facilitate communion among a range of local communities must not become a sort of formal superstructure over the local congregations.

> All eucharists and all bishops are local in character—at least in their primary sense. In a eucharistic view of the Church this means that the local Church, as defined earlier here, is the only form of ecclesial existence which can be properly called Church. All structures aiming at facilitating the universality of the Church create a *network of communion of Churches, not a new form of Church*. This is not only supported by history, but rests also upon sound theological and existential ground. Any structural universalization of the Church to the point of creating an ecclesial entity called "universal Church" as something parallel to or above that of the local Church would inevitably introduce into the concept

of the Church cultural and other dimensions which are foreign to a particular local context.[40]

The Free Churches

There is a growing consensus that the Christian churches seem to be drifting away from the traditional hierarchical model to more participative models of church organization.[41] Protestant Christianity seems to be moving toward a Free church format, and this movement has been called the "congregationalization" of the Christian churches, considered by some to be the fastest growing segment of Christianity. John Smyth (1554–1612) of Lincolnshire, England, gathered together the first congregation of Baptists, who were firmly committed to the practice of mature baptism, preceded by a personal declaration of faith on the part of the one to be baptized, rather than to infant baptism.[42] Smyth actually baptized himself because he insisted that there was in England no pure and spotless church to receive him. "In 1640 there were seven Baptist congregations in London, and forty-seven elsewhere in England, but many other Baptists were overseas, in Holland or New England."[43]

The Anabaptists and the liberal Reformed movements thought less of sacred Scripture and were more dependent on the direct influence of the Holy Spirit. The Quakers, founded by George Fox (1624–91), were convinced that there are no sacraments and no ministry, for God speaks in and through all believers. Each member of the faithful is able to have a direct relationship with God without the intervention of any priest or minister. Every believer has the right to minister as an equal partner with all the others. Yves Congar notes the following:

> The Friends [the Quakers] believe, then, that there are no sacraments and no ministry and that God speaks through and in all men. Even the history of the Bible as a sequence of events is of less value than the experience of the inner presence of God. They are convinced of the sacred character of each man, and that each man is capable of a personal, direct and autonomous relationship with God.[44]

Although special ministries are discouraged, most Free churches do have some ordained ministers, but "few if any Free churches understand ordination to be one of the sacraments as both Catholic churches [Roman Catholics and Orthodox] do. For most of them, ordination is just a public confirmation of a divine call already active in one's life."[45] An important characteristic of the Free churches is the overriding emphasis on the priesthood of all believers. According to Kärkkäinen, the Free churches prefer the church model revealed in 1 Corinthians to the model found in the Pastoral Epistles. Thus, they emphasize the mission of all the baptized over the specialized role of ordained ministers. A growing number of Christians do indeed view their religious affiliation as solely a matter between God and themselves. Miroslav Volf indicates that the early Baptists and the Methodists in the United States were as successful as they were because of their populist and democratic character.[46] In the religious sphere, there seems to be less and less enthusiasm for what Volf calls "top-down" organizations. Kärkkäinen observes that some of the more significant Free churches are the Quakers, the Congregationalists, the Baptists, and the Moravians.[47] Because of their rapid growth, the Free churches are considered equal participants in the ecumenical world with the Episcopal and Presbyterian churches. According to Volf, the Free churches represent the largest growing Protestant segment.[48]

The central emphasis of the Free churches is the local congregation. For them, there is no need for a bishop, for power resides in the full congregation. In fact, with a bishop in the church, the congregation actually loses its true nature as church. The Free church paradigm stresses the direct and immediate presence of Christ within the congregation. The limitation of the Free church model is that it tends to restrict the vision of its adherents to their own individual group and often fails to focus on the Christian worldwide mission. As the individual gathered assembly calls on the name of Christ as Lord, they do represent the whole church, and the universal church is realized through the addition or inclusion of the other churches. The Holy Spirit somehow brings them all together.

Volf insists that the primary identification of Free churches is the proclamation of the Word by every member of the gathered assembly.[49] He also affirms that baptism and the Lord's Supper are the essential rites of the majority of Free churches. He adds that any council or board above the existing churches is not of the essence of the church and should have no real power over the local Free churches. There can never be any subordination of the local assemblies to any presumed higher church authority. "Other churches, however, can intervene in the affairs of a local church only *if the ecclesiality of this church is threatened*. This is the case when the integral confession of faith is distorted in a church through the loss of the substance of faith or through permanent resistance in practice to Christ's rule (*status confessionis*)."[50] However, Volf adds the following:

> [A] congregation can indeed profess faith in Christ without positive connections with other congregations, but not in express isolation from them. By isolating itself from other churches, a

church attests either that it is professing faith in "a different Christ" than do the latter, or is denying in practice the common Jesus to whom it professes faith, the Christ who is, after all, the Savior and Lord of *all* churches, indeed of all the world.

This openness to all other churches is the *interecclesial minimum* of the concrete ecclesial proleptic experience of the eschatological gathering of the whole people of God.[51]

An attitude of openness to all the other churches is indispensable, although frequent dialogue with other congregations is by no means essential. Moreover, the Free churches' faith in Jesus as Lord necessitates an openness and an interest in the entire human race. It is important to note that any person who has faith in Christ should never be denied entrance to any of the Free churches.

All Christian believers have charismatic gifts and are expected to contribute to the church's life. Any marked division between those who serve and those who are served is not to be countenanced. Each believer has different and complementary gifts to contribute to the life of the church (1 Cor 12:7–11). Volf notes, however, that the majority of Free churches are open to the idea of ordained offices, although the charisms of office must be received and accepted by the entire congregation.[52] It is desirable for officeholders to be freely elected by the whole congregation.

Regarding the catholicity of the Free church, there is a growing consensus that a church is catholic inasmuch as the full range of spiritual gifts is available within it (Col 2:9–10). The Free churches acknowledge only the catholicity of the local churches because they accept no ecclesial reality other than the local community or church. Volf claims that an abiding openness to all other churches and loyalty to the apostolic tradition are the essential qualities of a church's catholicity.[53]

To understand the Free church ideology, it might be valuable to review briefly the ecclesiology of the Baptist theologian, Augustus Hopkins Strong, who taught at the Rochester Theological Seminary at the turn of the twentieth century. In his *Systematic Theology*, published in 1907, he deals with the constitution of the church.[54] He defines the church as an institution of divine appointment that is grounded in the social nature of man. It is a voluntary society and by no means an organization that necessitates or requires membership. Strong's position is that a specific form or shape of church polity is not in any way prescribed in the New Testament. Rather, expediency allows each body of believers to adopt a particular method of ecclesiastical structure that best suits its circumstances and conditions.[55]

Strong outlines his position as follows:

Any number of believers, therefore, may constitute themselves into a Christian church, by adopting for their rule of faith and practice Christ's law as laid down in the New Testament, and by associating themselves together, in accordance with it for his worship and service. It is important, where practicable, that a council of churches be previously called, to advise the brethren proposing this union to the desirableness of constituting a new and distinct local body; and, if it be found desirable, to recognize them, after its formation, as being a church of Christ. But such an action of a council, however valuable as affording ground for the fellowship of other churches, is not constitutive, but merely declaratory.[56]

Strong insists, however, that the absence of approval on the part of any other previously existing council of churches does not prevent such a new body of believers from being constituted as a true church of Christ.

In Strong's judgment, there is no evidence that Peter appointed the bishops of Rome as his successors, and even if he did appoint them, the evidence of continuous succession from the first century on is lacking. Furthermore according to Strong, "There is abundant evidence that a hierarchical form of church government is corrupting to the church and dishonoring to Christ.[57] However, this Baptist theologian does affirm the existence of two offices in the church, the office of bishop, presbyter, or pastor, and the office of deacon. Strong defines ordination as "the setting apart of a person divinely called to a work of special administration in the church."[58] This ordination does not involve the conferring of any special kind of power but simply acknowledges the capabilities conferred by God on the candidate. The ordination itself is actually a formal authorization to exercise the gifts already bestowed on the candidate by God.

The relationship of local Free churches to one another can be described as a fellowship among equals. This fellowship brings with it the duty to consult other local Free churches concerning matters that affect their common interest, such as common social action flowing out of the requirements of charity dictated in the New Testament.[59] Strong issues a final warning that this fellowship among the Free churches can be broken by clear and manifest departures from the faith or practice of the Scriptures on the part of any church.

The Baptist scholar James Wm. McClendon Jr. presents a more contemporary approach to ecclesiology in his *Systematic Theology*, published in 1994.[60] He locates his presentation within the plethora of contemporary treatises on the church, and he alleges that the variety of ecclesiologies has in some way contributed to the distancing of Christians, one from the other. He describes the phenomenon of ecumenism, beginning with the World Mission Conference in Edinburgh in 1910 and culminating in the formation of the World Council of Churches in 1948. These ecumenical developments have truly created a new climate of cooperation among Christians, although most Pentecostal bodies, the Southern Baptist Convention, and the Roman Catholic Church have been unwilling to participate fully in these gatherings.

According to McClendon, authentic *church* appears only when the Protestant members, Catholic representatives, and a new element, the Free churches, come together. In this convergence we experience what McClendon calls "full three-cornered witness to Christ."[61] Among Protestants it is easy to discern a strong local church element as well as a deepening emphasis on the Bible. This was a response, perhaps, to the Renaissance of the fourteenth and fifteenth centuries and its refinement of biblical scholarship. The Protestant movement was in part an outgrowth of this new cultural context.[62] The Reformers opted for simplicity of worship and were opposed to many of the medieval manifestations of church government and practice. Among Catholic believers, the sacramental and hierarchical structures continued to be most important, for that is how they have traditionally identified themselves. The episcopacy and the papacy remain in a true sense the rallying points of their church organization and polity, although each local church is said to contain the whole essential mystery of the church.

In McClendon's judgment, a new division had to be inserted because the Protestant and Catholic categories were no longer adequate. Among scholars it became clear that what McClendon calls "a separate stream of Christian existence" had to be recognized and identified. The Baptists, the Methodists, and later the Pentecostals had to be awarded separate treatment.[63] This third type of Christian community is predominantly local, mission oriented, and extremely conscious of the movements of the Spirit. There was a growing recognition at the beginning of the twentieth century that the church was changing, "for God is on the move and the end is not yet."[64] It also became increasingly clear that no type of Christian community is capable of simply absorbing the other two.

Moreover, McClendon is insistent that the three Christian branches remain open to the Jewish roots of Christianity and especially sensitive to the bitter experiences in the relations between Christians and Jews in the last two millennia. Somehow Christians must more deeply ground their ties with that early Jewish witness without which any united Christian endeavor would be incomplete.

In contrast to the Protestant and the Catholic components, McClendon calls the Free church segment the heir of the "radical reformation" that he relates to the Baptist tradition. This Free church grouping emphasizes Scripture reading, which serves as the foundation for the practice of mission, liberty, discipleship, and community.[65] The notion of the people of God offers a great incentive to unity among the three Christian segments. The principal marks of all the Christian communities are to be their worship and hospitality, their sharing of goods and their various ministries to the oppressed and the poor.

Christian leadership must be focused on Christ as the center and should not emphasize any heavy, overriding social control from church agencies above the local congregations. It envisions a fellowship that is built around the risen presence of Jesus. "From Spirit-gifted community practices comes the vector of a community that lives between the times, adapting, adjusting, transforming, interpreting so that the church can be the church even as it helps the world to see itself as world."[66] McClendon insists that in the churches the distinction between lay and clerical office has no New Testament roots. The development of hierarchical orders in the early centuries was radically deemphasized by the Reformers. The laity has become in many circles a second-rank Christian class, while the Pauline concept of charismatic gifts possessed by each believer has been largely lost in many communities.[67] There is to be a radical reformation in ministry where every member is called to a special, active role within the church. This should give full expression to the priesthood of all believers.

McClendon adds that Christian bodies such as the Roman Curia or the Southern Baptist Convention are to be considered agents and servants of each local church, meeting the urgent needs of the churches to clarify their own identity. However, such bodies must provide "an ecumenical open window through which the churches can reach out to one another in shared peoplehood, and beyond their own people, reach out to others in the Israel of God."[68]

The Pentecostals

The origins of Pentecostalism can be traced back to the Bethel Bible School in Topeka, Kansas, in 1901, and to the Azusa Street Mission in Los Angeles in the early years of the twentieth century. By 1950 or thereabouts, the movement began to appear in the more traditional churches. "The fact that the well known Pentecostal evangelist Oral Roberts joined the Methodist Church in 1968 is a significant indicator of the new direction of Pentecostalism, and may mark a turning point for the whole movement, old and new."[69] During the twentieth century, Pentecostalism became the largest single development in Protestantism.[70] "Pentecostalism . . . is still growing faster than any other Church. It is the strongest in the United

States and in South America, especially Chile. In Europe the biggest impact was made in Scandinavia, and Pentecostalism is now the largest Protestant body in Italy."[71]

The appearance of charismatic enthusiasm is more important to the Pentecostals than theological research and development. There are quite a number of species of Pentecostalism, and all are grounded in emotionalism, which expresses itself by means of speaking in tongues, prophesying, and healing. According to Veli-Matti Kärkkäinen, the principal tenets of Pentecostalism are justification by faith, the healing of the body, the return of Christ relatively soon, and baptism in the Holy Spirit as reflected in the speaking in tongues.[72] There are among the Pentecostals little interest and less agreement on the question of church organization, which for them can range from the pure congregational form to an episcopal structure. Pentecostalism can be considered a Christian revival movement with little interest in tradition or history.

The critical agent in the movement is the presence of the Holy Spirit, who aims to involve everyone in the mission of the local community. The Holiness Movement gained popularity in the United States in the nineteenth century at Ohio's Oberlin College. This movement concentrated on Spirit-baptism as distinct from water-baptism. There were then two baptisms, the first in water and the second in the Holy Spirit, which bestows on the subject the gift of tongues and prophecy.[73] Later, this second baptism came to be considered the occasion when one is especially empowered for service in the community. "In all these developments it has been the doctrine of baptism in the Holy Spirit which has been the center of attraction and the spear point of advance. . . . Any critical study of Pentecostalist theology must therefore inevitably center on that doctrine."[74]

Writing in 1995, Harvey Cox affirmed that Pentecostalism then embraced more than four hundred million people and was the fastest growing Christian movement on earth.[75] Membership in the United States includes blacks, whites, Asians, and Central Americans, largely from the less-privileged members of society. The movement grew out of widespread dissatisfaction with conventional religions, which seem to many to be nothing but an empty formality.[76] For Pentecostals, "the real enemy is the 'coldness' of conventional religion and the remoteness of God presented in the downtown churches."[77] Their principal emphasis is on the need for a personal experience of God and the development of what they term a primary spirituality. The rapid growth in the United States and in the Americas continued up to World War I and then exploded again after World War II.

The Pentecostals have normally been wary of organization and any heavy overlap of church structures. For them, the gift of tongues is the most critical gift of the Spirit. Speaking in tongues refers to a spiritual state of ecstasy that expresses itself in unintelligible sounds, thought to represent a direct manifestation of the Holy Spirit. This phenomenon goes back to the Montanists, who were a Christian revival movement in second century Phrygia (currently Turkey). But it is this emotional emphasis that is largely responsible for the exceptional growth of the movement. Cox says that around 1950, many observers were predicting the demise of Christianity as an organized religion, and it was at that very time that Pentecostalism broke forth around the globe. "As the twentieth century progressed, large blocks of people became increasingly skeptical about inherited religious dogmas, and ecclesiastical institutions steadily lost their power to shape cultures. . . . This is what gave the talk about secularization and the 'death of God' a certain plausibility."[78]

Catholics, Lutherans, and Methodists in significant numbers embraced the new movement and its emphasis on the emotional dimension of Christianity. Women have played an extremely important role in the growth of Pentecostalism everywhere. One of the great mysteries of the last one hundred years is how the worldwide expansion occurred so rapidly. Women like Aimee Semple McPherson (1890–1944) became very effective evangelists; they were the principal carriers of the fastest growing religious movement in the world.[79]

While many of the mainline Christian churches had been losing adherents in the latter 1900s, the Pentecostals continued to grow in places like South Korea, Africa, and Latin America. Although the growth of Pentecostalism has diminished somewhat among whites, its expansion among minorities in third world countries can be considered extraordinary. There has also been something of a change in the eschatology of the Pentecostals, from the anticipation of a fiery dissolution in the near future to a vision of the transformation of the earth into the promised kingdom.[80]

The Christian Century featured a number of valuable articles on the Pentecostals in its March 7, 2006, issue. Six brief studies summarize most of the recent information regarding the movement. Amos Yong, who teaches at the Regent University School of Divinity in Virginia, discusses the nature of the Pentecostal phenomenon, explaining that members have a more spiritualized rather than a predominantly institutionalized concept of church. He points out that the local churches are charged with the primary responsibility of introducing peace and justice into their world through the influence of the Holy Spirit.[81] The Pentecostals also provide a valuable service in vitalizing the sacramental and liturgical aspects of church life as revealed in the New Testament. The focal testimony that appears in Acts 1:8 has been complemented by other New Testament passages. Paul's epistles amplify the doctrinal dimensions of Pentecostal beliefs. For these adherents, however, the Acts of the Apostles remains their most important source of inspiration and direction, for the charismatic and mission developments found in Luke are for them extremely critical.

The Pentecostals are not particularly concerned about uniformity of church order and design since their emphasis is primarily on the diversity of individual gifts found among their members. Yong examines the various charisms of the Spirit that are operative in the Pentecostal churches. The function of the baptism of the Holy Spirit is to instill in believers a clear and vibrant witness to the power of the gospel, which they can promulgate within their world. The gift of healing also remains at the forefront of their mission. It is this gift of healing that touches great numbers of people and turns their focus on God. The Pentecostals are not especially interested in taking stands on doctrines such as the Trinity or the divine sonship of Jesus. They rather concentrate on truths such as the baptism of the Spirit.

Roger Olson, who teaches at the George W. Truett Theological Seminary at Baylor University, attests that there is within many of the Pentecostal communities a suspicion regarding scholars, both biblicists and theologians. In fact, a good many Pentecostal leaders are dubious about the value of their own scholars and their theological schools. This situation does, no doubt, retard the doctrinal development of the movement.[82]

The astronomical growth of Pentecostalism represents a phenomenon that almost defies statistical evaluation. The estimate of five to six hundred million adherents currently does not seem to be an exaggeration. Moreover, all of this growth has occurred roughly within a period of one hundred years. The missionary zeal of the Pentecostals has managed in that relatively short span of time to implant its message and its fervor literally throughout the world. It is appropriate to take note of the megachurches within the Pentecostal movement, although such huge congregations are also found among the Evangelicals. Harvey Cox observed in 1995 that megachurches are not at all uncommon in South Korea. "There may be no better way to grasp the astonishing scope and baffling complexity of Korean Pentecostalism than by paying a visit to the Yoido Full Gospel (Pentecostal) Church in Seoul, South Korea. This church is only a few decades old but has become the largest single Christian congregation on earth."[83]

According to Cox, this megachurch embraced eight hundred thousand members in 1995, and he emphasizes that its initial membership in 1958 had amounted to no more than five adherents. Cecil M. Robeck Jr., who teaches at Fuller Theological Seminary, describes a service at this church:

At Yoido Full Gospel Church in Seoul, reputedly the world's largest church, parishioners recite the Apostles' Creed, pray or sing the Lord's Prayer, and pray for the reunification of Korea every Sunday, reflecting something of the old Presbyterian majority. Preachers are expected to take off their shoes and don special slippers when they preach, for they stand on "holy ground." More pragmatically, during the service people are encouraged to pray aloud en masse in "concerts" of prayer, but prayer stops the second a bell is rung. American Pentecostals would find such things almost unthinkable."[84]

The doctrinal positions of the megachurches are difficult to describe because their teachings are quite general and lacking in detail. The same can be said concerning their worship ceremonies, which involve a great deal of vigorous music and call for frequent emotional responses. Miroslav Volf raises another serious issue with regard to the development of megachurches: "True, some of the churches are best described with a term meant as a compliment but that in fact comes dangerously close to being an insult—'successfully marketed churches.'"[85]

According to Philip Jenkins, a professor of history and religious studies at Pennsylvania State University, in the last forty years the Catholic Church has lost considerable ground in Latin America, and the Pentecostals conversely have expanded so dramatically that their growth has been called a new Reformation. "Since there were only a handful of Pentecostals in 1900, and several hundred million today, is it not reasonable to identify this as perhaps the most successful social movement of the past century? According to current projections, the number of Pentecostal believers should surpass the one billion mark before 2050."[86]

Notes

1. Rosemary Radford Ruether, *The Church Against Itself* (New York: Herder & Herder, 1967).
2. Ibid., 29.
3. Ibid., 52.
4. Ibid., 61.
5. Ibid., 85.
6. Ibid., 88.
7. Ibid., 90.
8. Ibid., 116.
9. Ibid., 120.
10. Ibid., 124.
11. Ibid., 127.
12. Ibid., 138.

13. Ibid., 164.
14. Ibid., 174.
15. Ibid., 185.
16. Rosemary Radford Ruether, *Women-Church: Theology in Practice* (San Francisco: Harper & Row, 1986).
17. Ibid., 5.
18. Ibid., 21.
19. Ibid., 27.
20. Ibid., 33.
21. Ibid., 34.
22. Ibid., 45.
23. Ibid., 56.
24. See Mary H. Snyder's critique of Rosemary Radford Ruether in *A New Handbook of Christian Theologians* (ed. D. W. Musser and J. L. Price; Nashville: Abingdon, 1996), 409.
25. John Meyendorff, *Byzantine Theology: Historical Trends and Doctrinal Themes* (New York: Fordham University Press, 1979), 91.
26. John Meyendorff, *The Byzantine Legacy in the Orthodox Church* (Crestwood, NY: St. Vladimir's Seminary Press, 1982), 222.
27. William La Due, *The Chair of Saint Peter* (Maryknoll, NY: Orbis, 1999), 80.
28. John Meyendorff, *Imperial Unity and Christian Divisions* (Crestwood, NY: St. Vladimir's Seminary Press, 1989), 327.
29. Meyendorff, *The Byzantine Legacy in the Orthodox Church*, 224.
30. John Meyendorff, *The Orthodox Church* (4th ed.; rev. by Nicholas Lossky; Crestwood, NY: St. Vladimir's Seminary Press, 1996), 200.
31. Ibid., 203.
32. John Meyendorff, "St. Peter in Byzantine Theology," in *The Primacy of Peter* (ed. John Meyendorff; Crestwood, NY: St. Vladimir's Seminary Press, 1992), 70.
33. Ibid., 81.
34. John D. Zizioulas, *Being as Communion* (Crestwood, NY: St. Vladimir's Seminary Press, 1985), 176.
35. Ibid., 185.
36. Ibid., 188.
37. Ibid., 226.
38. Ibid., 241.
39. Ibid., 254.
40. Ibid., 258.
41. Veli-Matti Kärkkäinen, *An Introduction to Ecclesiology: Ecumenical, Historical and Global Perspectives* (Downers Grove, IL: InterVarsity Press, 2002), 59. Kärkkäinen is a Finnish theologian, tenured at Fuller Theological Seminary

in Pasadena, California. In 2004, he was threatened with expulsion from the United States because he did not qualify under the new visa regulations for visiting religious professionals.

42. Kurt Aland, *A History of Christianity* (vol. 2; trans. James L. Schaaf; Philadelphia: Fortress, 1986), 475.

43. Owen Chadwick, *The Reformation* (1964; repr., New York: Viking Penguin, 1986), 207.

44. Yves Congar, *I Believe in the Holy Spirit* (vol. 1; trans. David Smith; New York: Seabury, 1983), 142.

45. Kärkkäinen, *An Introduction to Ecclesiology*, 65.

46. Miroslav Volf, *After Our Likeness: The Church as the Image of the Trinity* (Grand Rapids, MI: Eerdmans, 1998), 16. Volf is a Croatian-born theologian who is currently the director of the Yale Center for Faith and Culture.

47. Kärkkäinen, *An Introduction to Ecclesiology*, 64.

48. Volf, *After Our Likeness*, 20.

49. Ibid., 150.

50. Ibid., 155.

51. Ibid., 157.

52. Ibid., 249.

53. Ibid., 275.

54. Augustus Hopkins Strong, *Systematic Theology* (vol 3; Valley Forge, PA: Judson, 1907), 887.

55. Ibid., 896.

56. Ibid., 902.

57. Ibid., 911.

58. Ibid., 958.

59. Ibid., 926–27.

60. James Wm. McClendon Jr., *Doctrine: Systematic Theology* (vol. 2; Nashville, TN: Abingdon Press, 1994).

61. Ibid., 336.

62. Ibid., 337.

63. Ibid., 341.

64. Ibid., 344.

65. Ibid., 362.

66. Ibid., 367.

67. Ibid., 369.

68. Ibid., 370–71.

69. James D. G. Dunn, *The Christ and the Spirit* (vol. 2; Grand Rapids, MI: Eerdmans, 1996), 87.

70. Kärkkäinen, *An Introduction to Ecclesiology*, 69.

71. Dunn, *The Christ and the Spirit*, 86.

72. Kärkkäinen, *An Introduction to Ecclesiology*, 71.

73. Dunn, *The Christ and the Spirit*, 83.

74. Ibid., 88.

75. Harvey Cox, *Fire from Heaven* (1995; repr., Cambridge, MA: Da Capo Press, 2001), 15. The Victor Thomas Professor of Religion at Harvard, Cox became an overnight sensation with the publication of his book *The Secular City* in 1965. His study of Pentecostalism, *Fire from Heaven*, is a masterful presentation of the subject.

76. Ibid., 71.

77. Ibid., 75.

78. Ibid., 104.

79. Ibid., 137.

80. Ibid., 321.

81. Amos Yong, "Discerning the Spirit: Pentecostals in Theological Conversation," *The Christian Century*, March 7, 2006, p. 32.

82. Roger Olson, "Pentecostalism's Dark Side: Suspicions and Scandals," *The Christian Century*, March 7, 2006, p. 27.

83. Cox, *Fire from Heaven*, 219.

84. Cecil M. Robeck Jr., "Global and Local: Diverse Expressions," *The Christian Century*, March 7, 2006, p. 34.

85. Volf, *After Our Likeness*, 6.

86. Philip Jenkins, *The Next Christendom: The Coming of Global Christianity* (New York: Oxford University Press, 2002), 7–8.

BIBLIOGRAPHY

Aland, Kurt. *A History of Christianity*. Vol. 2. Translated by James L. Schaaf. Philadelphia: Fortress, 1986.

Alberigo, Giuseppe, et al. *Decrees of the Ecumenical Councils*. 2 vols. English editor, Norman P. Tanner. Washington, DC: Georgetown University Press, 1990.

Althaus, Paul. *The Theology of Martin Luther*. Translated by Robert C. Schultz. Philadelphia: Fortress, 1966.

Barraclough, Geoffrey. *The Medieval Papacy*. New York: Norton, 1968.

Barth, Karl. *The Doctrine of the Word of God*. Vol. 1, pt. 2 of *Church Dogmatics*. Translated by G. T. Thomson and H. Knight. New York: Scribner's, 1956.

———. *The Doctrine of Reconciliation*. Vol. 4, pt. 2 of *Church Dogmatics*. Translated by G. W. Bromiley. Edinburgh: T & T Clark, 1958.

———. *Church Dogmatics: A Selection*. Compiled and introduced by Helmut Gollwitzer. 1st American ed. Translated and edited by G. W. Bromiley. Louisville, KY: Westminster John Knox, 1994.

———. *Credo*. Foreword by Robert McAfee Brown. New York: Scribner's, 1962.

———. *The Epistle to the Romans*. Translated from the 1933 edition by Edwyn C. Hoskyns. New York: Oxford University Press, 1968.

———. *Evangelical Theology: An Introduction*. Translated from the 1963 edition by Grover Foley. Grand Rapids, MI: Eerdmans, 1986.

Baus, Karl. *From the Apostolic Community to Constantine*. Vol. 1. of *History of the Church*. Edited by Hubert Jedin and John Dolan. 1980. Repr., Tunbridge Wells: Burns & Oates, 1989.

Bernard of Clairvaux. *Five Books on Consideration*. Translated by J. Anderson and E. Kennan. Kalamazoo, MI: Cistercian Publications, 1976.

Boff, Leonardo. *Church: Charism and Power*. Translated by John W. Diercksmeier. New York: Crossroad, 1990.

———. *Ecclesiogenesis: The Base Communities Reinvent the Church*. Translated by Robert R. Barr. Maryknoll, NY: Orbis, 1986.

Bonhoeffer, Dietrich. *Discipleship*. Vol. 4 of *Dietrich Bonhoeffer Works*. 1937. Edited by Martin Kuske and Ilse Tödt. Translated by Barbara Green and Reinhard Krauss. English eds., Geffrey B. Kelly and John D. Godsey. Minneapolis, MN: Fortress, 2001. The original abridged English edition was published in 1949 as *The Cost of Discipleship*. A revised unabridged English edition of *The Cost of Discipleship* was published in 1959 by SCM and Macmillan.

———. *Letters and Papers from Prison*. Enl. ed. Edited by Eberhard Bethge. Incorporates text from the 1970 3d English ed. Edited by Reginald Fuller, Frank Clark, et al. Additional material by John Bowden. New York: Collier, 1972.

———. *Life Together and Prayerbook of the Bible*. Vol 5 of *Dietrich Bonhoeffer Works*. Translated by Daniel Bloesch and James H. Burtness from the 1987 German ed. English ed., Geffrey B. Kelly. Minneapolis: Fortress, 1996.

———. *Sanctorum Communio: A Theological Study of the Sociology of the Church*. Vol. 1 of *Dietrich Bonhoeffer Works*. Translated by Reinhard Krauss and Nancy Lukens from the 1960 German edition. English ed., Clifford J. Green. Minneapolis: Fortress, 1998.

Bouwsma, William J. *John Calvin: A Sixteenth Century Portrait*. New York: Oxford University Press, 1988.

Bowden, John. *Karl Barth: Theologian*. London: SCM, 1983.

Braaten, Carl E. *Mother Church: Ecclesiology and Ecumenism*. Minneapolis: Fortress, 1998.

Calvin, John. *Calvin's Institutes: A New Compend*. Edited by Hugh T. Kerr. Louisville, KY: Westminster John Knox, 1989.

Campenhausen, Hans von. *Ecclesiastical Authority and Spiritual Power in the Church of the First Three Centuries*. Translated by J. A. Baker. Stanford: Stanford University Press, 1969.

Chadwick, Owen. *The Reformation*. 1964. Repr., New York: Viking Penguin, 1986.

Congar, Yves M. J. *Diversity and Communion*. Translated by John Bowden. Mystic, CT: Twenty-Third Publications, 1985.

———. *Divided Christendom: A Catholic Study of the Problem of Reunion*. Translated by M. A. Bousfield. London: Geoffrey Bles/Centenary Press, 1939.

———. *Fifty Years of Catholic Theology: Conversations with Yves Congar*. Translated by John Bowden. Edited and introduced by Bernard Lauret. Philadelphia: Fortress, 1988.

———. "The Laity" and "The People of God." Session VI, 239–50, and Session V, 197–208, in *Vatican II: An Interfaith Appraisal*. Edited by John H. Miller. Notre Dame, IN: University of Notre Dame Press, 1966.

———. *Lay People in the Church*. Rev. ed. Translated by Donald Attwater. Westminster, MD: Newman Press, 1967.

————. *The Mystery of the Church: Studies by Yves Congar*. 2d rev. ed. Translated by Geoffrey Chapman, Ltd., and Helicon Press. Baltimore, MD: Helicon Press, 1960 and 1969.

————. *Power and Poverty in the Church*. Translated by Jennifer Nicholson. Baltimore, MD: Helicon Press, 1964.

————. *Vraie et Fausse Réforme dans L'Eglise*. Paris: Les Editions du Cerf, 1950.

Copleston, Frederick. *A History of Philosophy*. Vol. 3. Garden City, NY: Image Books, 1952.

Cox, Harvey. *Fire from Heaven*. 1995. Repr., Cambridge, MA: Da Capo Press, 2001.

Creeds of the Churches. 3d ed. Edited by John H. Leith. Louisville, KY: John Knox Press, 1982.

Cyprian of Carthage. *The Letters of St. Cyprian of Carthage*. Vol. 4. Translated by G. W. Clarke. In *Ancient Christian Writers* 47. Edited by Walter Burghardt and Thomas Lawler. New York: Newman Press, 1989.

————. *The Unity of the Catholic Church*. Translated by M. Bévenot. In *Ancient Christian Writers* 25. Edited by Johannes Quasten and Joseph Plumpe. New York: Newman Press, 1956.

de Gruchy, John W., ed. *The Cambridge Companion to Dietrich Bonhoeffer*. Cambridge, UK: Cambridge University Press, 1999.

A Democratic Catholic Church: The Reconstruction of Roman Catholicism. Edited by Eugene C. Bianchi and Rosemary Radford Ruether. New York: Crossroad, 1992.

Documents of the Christian Church. 3d ed. Edited by Henry Bettenson and Chris Maunder. Oxford: Oxford University Press, 1999.

Dunn, James D. G. *The Christ and the Spirit*. Vol. 2. Grand Rapids, MI: Eerdmans, 1996.

————. *Unity and Diversity in the New Testament*. 2d ed. London: SCM, 1990.

Erasmus, Desiderius. *Praise of Folly and Letter to Martin Dorp 1515*. Translated by Betty Radice. Introduction and notes by A. H. T. Levi. London: Penguin, 1971. Repr., 1987.

Fries, Heinrich, and Karl Rahner. *Unity of the Churches: An Actual Possibility*. Translated by Ruth C. L. Gritsch and Eric W. Gritsch. Philadelphia: Fortress, 1985.

Gerrish, B. A. *Continuing the Reformation*. Chicago: University of Chicago Press, 1993.

————. *The Old Protestantism and the New*. Chicago: University of Chicago Press, 1982.

————. *Tradition and the Modern World: Reformed Theology in the Nineteenth Century*. Chicago: University of Chicago Press, 1978.

Guy, John. *Tudor England*. Oxford: Oxford University Press, 1990.

Iserloh, Erwin. "The Reform in the German Principalities." In vol. 5 of
History of the Church. Edited by Hubert Jedin and John Dolan.
Translated by Anselm Biggs and Peter W. Becker. New York: Crossroad,
1990.
Jedin, Hubert, and John Dolan, eds. *History of the Church*. 10 vols. New
York: Crossroad, 1980–89.
Jenkins, Philip. *The Next Christendom: The Coming of Global Christianity*.
New York: Oxford University Press, 2002.
John of Paris. *On Royal and Papal Power*. Translated by J. A. Watt.
Toronto: Pontifical Institute of Mediaeval Studies, 1971.
Kärkkäinen, Veli-Matti. *An Introduction to Ecclesiology: Ecumenical,
Historical and Global Perspectives*. Downers Grove, IL: InterVarsity,
2002.
Küng, Hans. *Christianity: Essence, History and Future*. Translated by John
Bowden. New York: Continuum, 1995.
———. *The Church*. Translated by Ray and Rosaleen Ockenden. New
York: Sheed & Ward, 1967.
———. *Infallible? An Inquiry*. Translated by Edward Quinn. New York:
Doubleday, 1971.
———. *Infallible? An Unresolved Inquiry*. Translated by Edward Quinn.
New York: Continuum, 1994. This is an expanded version of
Infallible? An Inquiry.
———. *Reforming the Church Today*. Translated by Peter Heinegg with
Francis McDonagh, John Maxwell, Edward Quinn, and Arlene
Swidler. New York: Crossroad, 1990.
———. *Structures of the Church*. Translated by Salvator Attanasio. 1968.
Repr., New York: Crossroad, 1982.
———. *Theology for the Third Millennium: An Ecumenical View*.
Translated by Peter Heinegg. New York: Doubleday, 1988.
La Due, William. *The Chair of Saint Peter*. Maryknoll, NY: Orbis, 1999.
Latourette, Kenneth Scott. *Reformation to the Present: A.D. 1500–A.D.
1975*. Vol. 2 of *A History of Christianity*. Rev. ed.. San Francisco:
Harper & Row, 1975.
Lohse, Bernhard. *Martin Luther: An Introduction to His Life and Work*.
Translated by Robert C. Schultz. Philadelphia: Fortress, 1986.
Lortz, Joseph. *How the Reformation Came*. Translated by Otto M. Knab.
New York: Herder & Herder, 1964.
Luther, Martin. *Martin Luther's Basic Theological Writings*. Translated from
German and Latin. Edited by Timothy F. Lull. Minneapolis: Fortress,
1989.
———. *The Schmalkald Articles*. Translated by William R. Russell.
Minneapolis: Fortress, 1955.
Macquarrie, John. *The Faith of the People of God*. London: SCM, 1972.
———. *Principles of Christian Theology*. 2d ed. New York: Scribner's, 1977.

————. *Theology, Church and Ministry*. New York: Crossroad, 1986.

Marsilius of Padua. *Defensor Pacis*. Translated by Alan Gewirth. Toronto: University of Toronto Press, 1980.

Mask, E. Jeffrey. *At Liberty under God: Toward a Baptist Ecclesiology*. Lanham, MD: University Press of America, 1997.

McClendon, James Wm. Jr. *Doctrine*. Vol. 2 of *Systematic Theology*. Nashville, TN: Abingdon Press, 1994.

————. *Witness*. Vol. 3 of *Systematic Theology*. Nashville, TN: Abingdon Press, 2000.

McKelway, Alexander J. *The Systematic Theology of Paul Tillich*. Introductory report by Karl Barth. New York: Dell, 1964.

McNeill, John T. *The History and Character of Calvinism*. New York: Oxford University Press, 1954.

Meyendorff, John. *The Byzantine Legacy in the Orthodox Church*. Crestwood, NY: St. Vladimir's Seminary Press, 1982.

————. *Byzantine Theology: Historical Trends and Doctrinal Themes*. New York: Fordham University Press, 1979.

————. *The Orthodox Church*. 4th ed. Rev. and enl. by Nicholas Lossky. Crestwood, NY: St. Vladimir's Seminary Press, 1996.

————. *Rome, Constantinople, Moscow: Historical and Theological Studies*. Crestwood, NY: St. Vladimir's Seminary Press, 1996.

————. "St. Peter in Byzantine Theology." Pages 67–90 in *The Primacy of Peter*. Edited by John Meyendorff. Crestwood, NY: St. Vladimir's Seminary Press, 1992.

Moltmann, Jürgen. *The Church in the Power of the Spirit*. Translated by Margaret Kohl. London: SCM, 1977.

————. *The Open Church*. Translated by M. Douglas Meeks. London: SCM, 1978.

Morris, Colin. *The Papal Monarchy: The Western Church from 1050–1250*. Oxford: Clarendon Press, 1989.

Nichols, Aidan. *Yves Congar*. Wilton, CT: Morehouse-Barlow, 1989.

Noble, Thomas F. X. *The Republic of St. Peter: The Birth of the Papal State, 680–825*. Philadelphia: University of Pennsylvania Press, 1984.

Oberman, Heiko A. *Luther: Man between God and the Devil*. Translated by Eileen Walliser-Schwarzbart. New Haven: Yale University Press, 1989.

————. *The Two Reformations*. Edited by Donald Weinstein. New Haven: Yale University Press, 2003.

O'Grady, Colm. *The Church in the Theology of Karl Barth*. Washington, DC: Corpus Books, 1968.

Olin, John C. *Catholic Reform*. New York: Fordham University Press, 1990.

Olson, Roger. "Pentecostalism's Dark Side: Suspicions and Scandals." *The Christian Century* (March 7, 2006): 27–30.

Ostrogorsky, George. *The History of the Byzantine State.* Translated by Joan Hussey. 1952. Repr., New Brunswick, NJ: Rutgers University Press, 1969.

Outler, Albert C. *The Wesleyan Theological Heritage: Essays of Albert C. Outler.* Introduced and edited by Thomas Oden and Leicester Longden. Grand Rapids, MI: Zondervan, 1991.

Ozment, Steven. *The Age of Reform 1250–1550.* New Haven: Yale University Press, 1980.

Pannenberg, Wolfhart. *The Church.* Translated by Keith Crim. Philadelphia: Westminster, 1983.

———. *Systematic Theology.* Vol. 3. Translated by Geoffrey W. Bromiley. Grand Rapids, MI: Eerdmans, 1998.

Pauck, Wilhelm. *From Luther to Tillich.* Edited by Marion Pauck. San Francisco: Harper & Row, 1984.

Pauck, Wilhelm and Marion. *Paul Tillich: His Life and Thought.* San Francisco: Harper & Row, 1989.

Pelikan, Jaroslav. *Christian Doctrine and Modern Culture (since 1700).* Vol. 5 of *The Christian Tradition.* Chicago: University of Chicago Press, 1989.

———. *Reformation of Church and Dogma (1300–1700).* Vol. 4 of *The Christian Tradition.* Chicago: University of Chicago Press, 1984.

———. *The Spirit of Eastern Christendom (600–1700).* Vol. 2 of *The Christian Tradition.* Chicago: University of Chicago Press, 1974.

Rahner, Karl. *Foundations of Christian Faith: An Introduction to the Idea of Christianity.* Translated by William V. Dych. New York: Crossroad, 1986.

———. *The Shape of the Church to Come.* Translated and introduced by Edward Quinn. London: SPCK, 1974.

———. *Theology of Pastoral Action.* Translated by W. J. O'Hara. English adaptation by Daniel Morrissey. New York: Herder & Herder, 1968.

Renouard, Yves. *The Avignon Papacy.* Translated by D. Bethell. New York: Barnes & Noble, 1970.

Roark, Dallas M. *Dietrich Bonhoeffer.* Waco, TX: Word, 1972.

Robeck, Cecil M. Jr. "Global and Local: Diverse Expressions." *The Christian Century* (March 7, 2006): 34.

Robinson, John A. T. *Honest to God.* London: SCM, 1963.

———. *The New Reformation?* Philadelphia: Westminster, 1965.

———. *On Being the Church in the World.* London: SCM, 1960; Pelican Books, 1969.

Ruether, Rosemary Radford. *The Church Against Itself.* New York: Herder & Herder, 1967.

———. *Women-Church: Theology in Practice.* San Francisco: Harper & Row, 1986.

Runciman, Steven. *The Eastern Schism.* Oxford: Clarendon Press, 1955.

Schleiermacher, Friedrich. *The Christian Faith*. Translated from the 2d German ed. Edited by H. R. MacKintosh and J. S. Stewart. Edinburgh: T&T Clark, 1986.

————. *On Religion: Speeches to Its Cultured Despisers*. Edited and translated by Richard Crouter. Cambridge, UK: Cambridge University Press, 1988; repr., 2000.

Schmemann, Alexander. "A Response to the *Decree on Eastern Catholic Churches*." In *The Documents of Vatican II*. Edited by Walter M. Abbott. New York: Herder & Herder, 1966.

Scott, William A. *Historical Protestantism: An Historical Introduction to Protestant Theology*. Englewood Cliffs, NJ: Prentice-Hall, 1971.

Spitz, Lewis W., ed. *The Protestant Reformation, 1517–1559*. New York: Harper & Row, 1985.

Strong, Augustus Hopkins. *Systematic Theology: A Compendium*. Valley Forge, PA: Judson, 1907.

Taylor, Mark Kline. *Paul Tillich: Theologian of the Boundaries*. London: Collins Liturgical Publications, 1987.

Tierney, Brian. *Church Law and Constitutional Thought in the Middle Ages*. London: Variorum Reprints, 1979.

————. *Foundations of the Conciliar Theory*. Cambridge, MA: Cambridge University Press, 1955.

The Thought of Paul Tillich. Edited by James Luther Adams, Wilhelm Pauck, and Roger Lincoln Shinn. San Francisco: Harper & Row, 1985.

Tillich, Paul. *The New Being*. New York: Scribner's, 1955.

————. *The Protestant Era*. Abridged ed. Translated by James Luther Adams. Chicago: University of Chicago Press, 1957.

————. *The Shaking of the Foundations*. New York: Scribner's, 1948.

————. *Systematic Theology*. 3 vols. in one. Chicago: University of Chicago Press, 1967.

The Treatise on the Apostolic Tradition of St. Hippolytus of Rome. Edited by Gregory Dix and Henry Chadwick. Repr., London: Alban Press, 1992.

Ullmann, Walter. *The Growth of Papal Government in the Middle Ages*. 3d ed. 1955. Repr., Northampton, UK: John Dickens & Co., 1970.

————. *A Short History of the Papacy in the Middle Ages*. 1972. Repr. with additions, New York: Methuen, 1982.

Volf, Miroslav. *After Our Likeness: The Church as the Image of the Trinity*. Grand Rapids, MI: Eerdmans, 1998.

Wolter, Hans. "Heresy and the Beginnings of the Inquisition." In vol. 4 of *History of the Church*. Edited by Hubert Jedin and John Dolan. Translated by Anselm Biggs. New York: Crossroad, 1986.

Yong, Amos. "Discerning the Spirit: Pentecostals in Theological Conversation." *The Christian Century* (March 7, 2006): 31–33.

Zizioulas, John D. *Being as Communion*. Crestwood, NY: St. Vladimir's Seminary Press, 1985.

INDEX